HOLT BASIC EDUCATION PROGRAM

FIRST SERIES   *(Zero through 4th Grade Reading Level)*
LEARNING TO READ AND WRITE
LEARNING TO WRITE (workbook)
LIFE WITH THE LUCKETTS
THE THOMASES LIVE HERE
GET YOUR MONEY'S WORTH
MEASURE, CUT, AND SEW

INTERMEDIATE SERIES   *(Elementary School Subjects)*
● AMERICAN HISTORY
ARITHMETIC
BASIC DICTIONARY OF AMERICAN ENGLISH
ENGLISH II
IMPRESSIONS OF THE UNITED STATES
INTRODUCTION TO GEOGRAPHY
SCIENCE

ADVANCED SERIES   *(Pre-High School Subjects)*
BIOLOGICAL SCIENCE
EARTH AND SPACE SCIENCE
PHYSICAL SCIENCE
ENGLISH III
FUNDAMENTAL MATHEMATICS
PRINCIPLES OF GEOGRAPHY
YOU AND THE LAW

American History

George D. Crothers, Ph. D.

CBS News

 Holt, Rinehart and Winston, Inc., New York

ACKNOWLEDGMENT

Grateful acknowledgment is made for the assistance and advice generously given by the State Directors of Adult Education, the U. S. Office of Education, and other leaders of Adult Education in planning the Holt Basic Education Program.

Contents

Introduction

This book will help to explain what America is, and what is meant by the "American Way of Life." It is the story of how Americans learned to think and act the way they do, and how they made the United States the country it is today.

CHAPTER 1

Discovery and Settlement

AMERICA WAS DISCOVERED IN THE YEAR 1492

The United States is a young country. Five hundred years
ago Indians in North America hunted in the forests and lived
in scattered villages. These Indians did not know how to read
or write. They made only the simplest tools. They had little
trade or business. There were no cities. And there were no
white men in North America at all.

White men who lived in Europe did not even know that
America was here. Then, in the year 1492, an Italian sea cap-
tain discovered it by accident. The captain, Christopher
Columbus, was employed by the King and Queen of Spain.

The Spanish rulers wanted their businessmen to share in
the rich trade with India and the Far East. In India Europeans mostly bought spices, perfumes and silks. Spices made
dried meats and vegetables taste much better. Perfumes
were used in those days as a substitute for bath soap. And

1

silk cloth was thought to be more elegant than wool or linen.

But Italians and Arabs kept everyone else away from the regular trade routes. Brave Portuguese sailors sailed south along the coast of Africa looking for a new way to India. Columbus sailed straight west across the Atlantic Ocean. He found islands in the Caribbean Sea. Thinking that he was in India, he called these islands the *Indies*. He called the natives on the islands Indians.

Spanish, French and English Explorers Followed Columbus

Soon Spaniards began to explore the New World. Cortez and a few soldiers conquered the rich Aztec Indians in Mexico. Balboa discovered the Pacific Ocean. Pizzaro crossed the Andes Mountains and took over the wealth of the Inca Indians in Peru. Silver taken from the mines in Mexico and Peru made Spain a rich country. Spanish governors and missionaries followed the conquerors and explorers. Soon Spain ruled Mexico, Florida and most of Central and South America. However, not many Spanish families came to live in the New World.

During the hundred years after the voyage of Columbus, French and English seamen explored both the coasts of North America. But they did not settle any place in the New World. Sir Walter Raleigh, an Englishman, tried to set up a colony in what is now North Carolina. However, the colony did not prosper. By the time an English ship arrived to take the colonists home, everyone had died.

THE FIRST ENGLISH SETTLEMENT WAS IN VIRGINIA

Meanwhile England was growing stronger. English sea captains robbed Spanish ships. And in 1588 the English defeated Spain's great navy. English businessmen formed large companies to trade with Russia and India. Other businessmen had enough money to set up a colony in America.

2

In 1607 the English organized a company for this purpose. It was called the Virginia Company. It had a charter from the king. Businessmen put up the money. Other men, called settlers, agreed to live and work in the colony. They all hoped to find gold and silver as the Spaniards had. They also wanted to claim American land for England before Spain got it all. In addition, some of them hoped to convert the Indians to Christianity.

The charter gave the company all business and trading rights in America from Virginia to Maine. It gave the company the right to rule in the name of the English king. But the company had to rule according to English law. Settlers kept their rights as English citizens. They could not be arrested without good reason and they had the right to a trial by jury.

The first ships landed at Jamestown in Virginia and the settlers built a fort. But they found no gold or silver. Many got sick and died. Others starved. Some Indians helped the settlers, but other Indians fought them. Often the settlers were cruel to the Indians.

Each year more men were sent to Virginia. The settlers learned to plant their own crops and stopped looking for gold. Life in the colony improved. Settlers began to grow tobacco which they could sell for a profit in England. Then the company allowed settlers to own their own land. Thus the settlers became independent businessmen. Women started to arrive in Virginia and family life began.

The House of Burgesses Was Set Up to Make Local Laws

The settlers did not always agree with the company's rules about taxes, money payments and land. They wanted a voice in these affairs. So the company set up a local lawmaking body in Virginia called the House of Burgesses. The settlers elected men to represent them in this lawmaking body. This made the colony partly self-governing. However, they did not elect their governor. He was appointed by the company.

The company never made money, and in 1624 the English king took over the colony. Now the king, instead of the company, appointed the governor. But the House of Burgesses continued to make local laws.

Years later when other colonies were started, their governments were much like that of Virginia. Sometimes, as in the case of North Carolina and South Carolina, the King of England gave charters to a few of his noblemen friends. In Maryland and in Pennsylvania, he gave a charter to single persons. Such men were known as *proprietors,* and their colonies were known as proprietary colonies. The proprietor always appointed the governor in his colony, but there was a local assembly made up of men elected by the settlers. These representatives dealt with local matters. Often they quarreled with the governor.

SOME SETTLEMENTS WERE BEGUN FOR RELIGIOUS REASONS

When Columbus sailed for America in 1492, almost everybody in Western Europe was a member of the Roman Catholic Church. People called Turks, who were not Christians, ruled in parts of Eastern Europe.

There were Jewish people in Europe, but they were "segregated" and they were not given equal rights. Jews were not even allowed to live in England. And in the same year that Columbus discovered America, all Jews were forced to leave Spain.

Leaders of the Roman Catholic Church made rules about religion that many people did not like. Some leaders grew careless and a few of them were bad. They refused to admit their mistakes, and they failed to clean up the church government. Many men, like the German monk Martin Luther, wanted reforms. Luther was put out of the church in 1520. But the local government in Germany helped Luther and refused to punish him even though the church insisted on it. Many people followed Luther and other reformers. They formed new churches. These people were called *Protestants*. Protestants wanted to worship God in one way, Catholics in another way. Each group tried to make the other agree with it. They did not believe it was right to worship differently and still live together in one country. They fought wars over religion. Some countries, such as England, Holland, Northern Germany and Sweden, became Protestant. France, Italy and Spain remained Roman Catholic.

Then Protestants began to disagree with one another. In England the Christian church became Protestant by order of the king. There were people, however, who thought that the church was not Protestant enough. They wanted to do away with some of its practices and "purify" the church. People who felt this way were called Puritans. A few of the Puritans who were very strict about worship wanted to separate from the English church. They thought they would be able to worship in their own way in Holland. When that did not work out, they decided to move to the New World. These people were called Pilgrims.

The Pilgrims Set Up the Plymouth Colony

The Pilgrims agreed with a business company called the Plymouth Company that they would go to the New World as settlers. This company, like the Virginia Company, had a charter from the King of England. In the year 1620 the Pilgrims sailed from Plymouth, England, in a small ship named the *Mayflower*. They took their wives and children.

The *Mayflower* was supposed to land near Virginia. Instead, the ship was blown northward. It finally anchored off the coast of Massachusetts. This meant that the Pilgrims landed in a place that was far from the Virginia settlement. Therefore, the Pilgrims had to make their own laws. Not everyone on the *Mayflower* was a Pilgrim. The company had

5

hired extra men to do all the different jobs that were needed. But all the men agreed that once ashore they would make and obey their own laws. Their agreement is called the Mayflower Compact. The men elected their own governor, and for many years their governor was William Bradford.

When the Pilgrims went ashore they built log huts. It was November and bitter cold. There was not enough food. Many of the Pilgrims got sick and died, but other families survived. Their colony was called Plymouth, and it became a village where men governed themselves. Everybody in the colony worshiped as the Pilgrims did.

The Massachusetts Bay Colony Was Founded by Other Puritans

Ten years later other Puritans formed a new company, the Massachusetts Bay Company. They raised money in England, and sent Puritan families to settle where Boston is now. Within two years, 2,000 people came to live in Boston and nearby Salem. All of the leaders were Puritans, so everybody had to worship as the Puritan leaders did.

Even in Boston, however, the Puritans could not agree. One man, Roger Williams, said he did not have to believe exactly as the others did. All the leaders felt that Williams was wrong, and they forced him to leave Boston. Williams walked eighty miles through the woods in mid-winter to Rhode Island. Here he began a new colony where anyone could worship as he pleased. He called his new colony Providence. Thus Rhode Island became the first English colony in which more than one religion was allowed.

Catholics Founded Maryland and Quakers Founded Pennsylvania

In 1634 the colony of Maryland was settled by an English nobleman named Lord Baltimore. At that time, life in England was difficult for Catholics because they would not join

the Church of England. Because his son was a Catholic, Lord Baltimore set up Maryland as a place where Catholics could worship in peace. He also allowed Protestants to live in the colony. However, only Christians were given the right to worship as they pleased. Living side by side, Protestants and Catholics often quarreled. But clearing the land and getting food seemed more important than religious differences. In the end, Protestants and Catholics learned to accept one another.

The colony of Pennsylvania was founded by William Penn in 1681. Penn belonged to the Religious Society of Friends, or Quakers. In England, Quakers were treated almost as though they were outlaws. But Penn was the son of a famous British admiral to whom the king owed money. To pay his debt, the king gave William Penn rights as proprietor in America west of the Delaware River. In Philadelphia, Penn built a settlement where Quakers would be welcome. Quakers had suffered because of the laws against them, so they did not make laws against other religions. In Pennsylvania men were free to worship as they pleased.

SOME COLONIES WERE SETTLED FOR OTHER REASONS

New York was not begun by the English, but by the Dutch. Merchants in the Netherlands had trading posts on the Hudson River even before the Puritans came to Boston. New Amsterdam, as they called it, became a busy Dutch colony. Men of many nations and many different religions settled there. Jews were admitted in 1623.

England won a war against the Dutch in 1664 and took over New Amsterdam. The king gave the colony to his brother, the Duke of York, and it was renamed New York. Part of this colony, now New Jersey, was given to two other proprietors.

Delaware, too, was not founded by the English. A trading

company from Sweden founded it in 1638. The Dutch took it from the Swedes, and then the English took it away from the Dutch.

Connecticut was founded by people from Massachusetts who settled in Hartford. These people wanted more freedom of worship than the Puritan leaders of Boston would give them. They also wanted more land and a stronger voice in local affairs than they had been granted in Boston. Other families came directly from England to settle in places like New Haven. Together these groups set up a colony that would govern itself.

New Hampshire was founded by men from Boston who moved north to farm and fish and trade. New Hampshire became a royal colony in 1680.

Far to the south, Georgia was founded in 1733 by James Oglethorpe, a proprietor who wanted to set up a refuge for debtors. In 1752 Georgia also became a royal colony.

EACH BRITISH COLONY HAD AN ASSEMBLY TO VOTE ON LOCAL LAWS

By this time there were thirteen British colonies in North America. They all had governments very much alike. Only two colonies, Connecticut and Rhode Island, could govern themselves and elect their own governors. The other colonies had governors who were appointed by the king or by proprietors. Each governor appointed a council. But in every colony there was an assembly of representatives elected by the colonists to vote on local taxes and local laws. Thus the colonists had years of practice in self-government.

In each colony it was agreed more and more that men had a right to worship as they pleased. In Virginia and Massachusetts the church was part of the government, but even in these colonies many denominations were allowed. The idea of religious freedom grew both in theory and in practice.

REVIEW ACTIVITIES

1. Why were Europeans interested in finding a new trade route to India?
2. Give three reasons why the English wished to set up a colony in Virginia.
3. Who were the Pilgrims? Why did they leave England?
4. Why did Roger Williams leave Boston? What colony did he set up?
5. By 1752, all of the British colonies had similar governments. Describe these governments.

Select the words that best complete the following sentences. (*Please do not write in this book.*)

1. A Spanish soldier named _____ conquered the Aztec Indians who lived in _____.
2. In 1607, a group of English businessmen started the _____ Company. The king gave these men a _____ that said they could set up a colony and trade in North America.
3. The colony of _____ was founded by Lord Baltimore as a place where _____ could worship in peace.
4. The colony of _____ was founded by William Penn as a settlement where _____ would be welcome.
5. _____ _____ became a British colony after the English took it from the Dutch in 1664. Under the Dutch the colony had been called _____ _____.

Who or what were the following:

1. Sir Walter Raleigh
2. Proprietor
3. House of Burgesses
4. Mayflower Compact
5. James Oglethorpe

CHAPTER 2

Colonial Development

THE COLONIES OFFERED FREEDOM AND OPPORTUNITIES

The British colonies in America grew rapidly. Within a century and a half more than 750,000 men and women had left their homes in England and Europe to settle in the new land. They crossed the dangerous ocean in small ships to face hard work, wilderness and disease. Why did they do it?

Some came so they would be free to worship as they chose. A few came to make money for a trading company. Almost all hoped to have more food and better shelter than before. In England the landowners had begun to use farmland for raising sheep. Farmers were often put off the land and there were many men who could not find jobs. Scotch-Protestants who lived in North Ireland paid heavy taxes, and English laws cut into their profit from trade and manufacture. So there was unemployment in North Ireland. In a single year 10,000 immigrants arrived in America from Belfast alone!

In Germany and France, wars over politics and religion resulted in heavy taxes. Marching armies ruined farms. Young men were taken off their land and forced into hard military service. To escape from all this and to worship in their own way, many Germans came to live in America—especially in Pennsylvania.

Most newcomers paid for their own expenses. Some agreed to work as a kind of slave for a few years if someone would pay their travel costs. After five or seven years they were free. Everyone became part of a growing country.

In America there was land for everyone. A man could be independent on a farm of his own. Many settlers would rather chop down trees and plant crops than work for wages. As a result, labor was always scarce in the seaboard towns and wages were higher in America than in Europe.

Boston, New York and Philadelphia became young cities and busy seaports. Ships brought clothing, tools and manufactured goods from England. They took back furs, grain, dyes, naval supplies and tobacco. American colonists sent grain and salt meat to the West Indies and brought back molasses. No real unemployment existed. Food and shelter were available for all who worked. Large families were the rule. By 1775 more than 2 million people were living in the American colonies.

Local Self-Government Began Early

Life in America meant hard work, but life was prosperous. It was also free. Many colonists came to America in order to escape from laws that they disliked. In the new land, they made their own local laws. Except for the early years when Puritan leaders in Massachusetts and royal governors in Virginia ruled strictly, the settlers had a big voice in their government.

In New England each new town governed itself through meetings of all settlers who owned property in that town.

Every town also elected men to the colonial assembly where larger matters were dealt with. In the South officials of each parish were elected locally, and county officials were appointed from among the local landowners. Farther west on the frontier, there was hardly any government at all. Men were left alone to cope with the problems of nature and the threat of unfriendly Indians.

Men grew used to this kind of self-government and freedom. They came to believe that laws that did not suit them were bad, and they thought they had a right to change them.

Settlers Moving West Had Little Voice in Local Government

The settlers who moved west from the first seaboard towns did not have a fair share in the making of local laws. Furthermore, the colonies as a whole had no share in the making of laws for the British Empire.

As the colonies grew larger and new settlers moved west, the newcomers often did not like the laws made by the old settlers. They demanded a voice in the framing of laws. Sometimes they succeeded; sometimes they did not.

Only one year after the first large Puritan settlement was started in Boston, families who had settled in Watertown, five miles away, found that the Puritan governor in Boston taxed them without their consent. They protested and the governor had to let each Massachusetts town send two representatives to the General Court.

Years later, planters in Virginia who had moved west had little voice in the House of Burgesses. They paid taxes, but the governor would not help to defend them against the Indians. In 1676, led by a man named Nathaniel Bacon, they took control of the colony's government by force. For a time they ruled the colony themselves, but the royal government got control again. A hundred years later there was a similar uprising in North Carolina.

In nearly every colony, people who lived in the seaboard

area were in control of the government. Frontiersmen in Pennsylvania complained that while three counties around Philadelphia elected twenty-six members of the legislature, the five western counties elected only ten. In Virginia 19,000 men living in the tidewater, or coastal, areas had more votes than 30,000 men who lived in the western counties. Of course the laws and the tax rates favored the seaboard towns. Westerners did not like this.

Although western settlers did not trust the richer colonists in the cities, all colonists disliked many of the laws that were imposed on them by the English king and Parliament. Parliament was the lawmaking body of England.

THE COLONISTS OPPOSED MANY ENGLISH LAWS

The American colonists were British subjects. They were part of the British Empire and they owed allegiance to the King of England.

But the king and Parliament believed that the empire existed for the good of England, the mother country. They thought it only proper to consider England more important than any of her colonies. So the English laws about defense, government, manufacture and trade were for England first and for the colonies second. Many of these laws were good for the colonies. Some of them, however, did not serve the interests of those people living in America. It was because of these laws that the colonists said Parliament had no right to interfere with colonial affairs.

Most of the disagreements were over laws about trade and manufacture and over taxes for defense.

England Tried to Control All Trade with Her Colonies

In those days the idea about trade and manufacture was roughly this: There is only a certain amount of manufacturing and trading that can be done in the world; so the more manufacturing and trading a nation does for itself, the more money it will make, and the stronger it will be. For England to do this, she had to prevent foreign countries from sharing in English trade and manufacture. And she had to win as much trade with foreign countries as she could. This was known as having a "favorable balance of trade."

Soon after the colonies were founded, England's big rival for trade was the Netherlands. Dutch shipowners bought tobacco in Virginia and sold it in Europe. The profit they made stayed in Holland. According to the thinking of English rulers, the profit should have gone to England. So as early as 1621 a law of England stated that all tobacco from British colonies had to be shipped to England. It also stated that Englishmen could buy tobacco only from British colonies. Because this gave American tobacco growers a sure market, it seemed fair. Later, an English law said that *all* goods shipped to England from any place in the world had to arrive on English ships. This kept Dutch ships out of England and it created a need for more English ships. Since any ships built in the American colonies were considered English, a profitable shipbuilding industry grew in New England to meet this market.

Later on, other goods were made subject to the same rules as tobacco. After 1660 the colonies could ship sugar, cotton, dyes and a long list of other goods only to England. In return, English merchants could buy these goods only from the colonists.

Such laws created no great hardship for the colonists, and they gave them some advantages. But they did keep Americans from buying and selling directly in Europe where they could get higher prices. This was irritating. New England shippers refused to obey the English shipping rules, so the king took away Massachusetts's charter and made it a royal colony. The king then appointed a royal governor to enforce his laws.

The colonists had other reasons to be dissatisfied. British merchants paid low prices for American produce, but they sold their own goods to Americans for high prices. Thus the colonists were always short of cash. While British merchants got rich, colonists found it hard to do business locally. The colonists wanted to coin money in America or print their own paper money. But Parliament would never let them do this.

Other British rules and regulations seemed equally unfair to the colonists. One of these was a regulation in 1733 which said that colonists could buy molasses only from other British colonies. The colonists in New England bought a lot of molasses, from which they made rum. If they wanted to buy molasses from Spanish or French islands in the West Indies, first they had to have it shipped to England. Otherwise they had to pay a very high tax on it. If the Americans observed this law, it would cost them a lot of money. So they evaded the law and became smugglers. Fortunately for them, the law was not strictly enforced. But it was the kind of law that the colonists thought was unfair.

The British government also put limits on American manufacture. Parliament forbade Americans to make or sell woolen goods, to export hats, or to make anything out of iron. If Americans wanted such things, said Parliament, they must buy them from England. The British did not want industry in America to compete with her own industry.

THE COLONIAL GOVERNORS HAD STRONG POWERS

Colonial governors tried to enforce all the rules on trade and manufacture. This made them very unpopular. But royal and proprietary governors were powerful. They appointed—and they could also dismiss—all judges and all government officials who enforced the laws.

Freedom of the Press Was Upheld in the Zenger Trial

Once, when the Governor of New York dismissed a judge, a publisher named John Peter Zenger criticized the governor in print. The governor said that this was the same as an attack on the king. He sued Zenger in court. But Zenger had a good lawyer, Andrew Hamilton, of Philadelphia. Hamilton argued that since Zenger had only printed the truth, he was not guilty of libel. The jury set Zenger free. This famous case was one of the most important steps toward freedom of the press in America.

Colonial Assemblies Sometimes Opposed the Governors

Colonial governors acted like kings. The governor called the assembly together, and he could also send the assembly home. He had the power to veto any act passed by the colonial assembly. The colonists grew to dislike the idea of an executive who was stronger than the legislature. Sometimes they refused to raise money for the governor's salary. And often they refused to co-operate with officials of the king.

Such disputes continued for a long time. After 1760 they became more serious.

WARS MADE THE BRITISH EMPIRE BIGGER

The English won a war with the Dutch over trading rights. In 1664 they took over the Dutch colonies in America. Then the English joined in European wars against France. In the seventy-five years before 1763, England fought four very long wars against France. France controlled what is now Canada and the entire Mississippi River valley. These French settlements were close to the British colonies, but American colonists did not take much part in the fighting until the last war. This one, fought from 1755 to 1763, is known in America as the French and Indian War.

England and France Fought for Control of North America

The fight for control of North America began when the French moved into western Pennsylvania. The Governor of Virginia sent troops commanded by George Washington, a Virginia planter, to oppose them. However, this small Virginia force was driven back. The French built a fort where Pittsburgh is now. An English army under General Braddock was sent to capture it, but the English were badly beaten by the French and Indians.

The French also captured forts in western and northern New York. This was serious, and representatives of the British colonies met at Albany to see what could be done about it. They planned to unite all of the colonies for the purpose of defense. However, the plan was voted down by both the Americans and the British.

Meanwhile, England sent a larger army that captured Quebec in Canada in 1759. The other French armies in America were cut off from their source of supplies, and they had to surrender. The French and Indian War ended in 1763, and England won. France had to give up all of her settlements in Canada and all the land she held east of the Mississippi River.

Now the British colonies in America were safe from French attack. There was more land to settle. The population was growing. American trade and manufacture were increasing in spite of the British regulations. But the colonists still disagreed with many of the laws that were passed by Parliament. They thought that England ignored American interests. And they resented the great power of the colonial governors who enforced the English laws.

By this time the British Empire had grown very large. England wanted to run the empire for a profit. Consequently, English rule in America became more and more severe. This led to trouble.

REVIEW ACTIVITIES

1. Give four reasons why settlers came from England and Europe to settle in the New World.
2. Why did the colonists oppose many of England's laws? What did they do about them?
3. Why did England regulate American trade?
4. Why was Massachusetts made a royal colony?
5. How did the French and Indian War begin? What was its outcome?

Select the words that best complete the following sentences. (*Please do not write in this book.*)

1. German colonists settled mostly in _____.
2. _____ settlers had fewer representatives in the colonial assemblies than the people in _____ towns.
3. British merchants paid _____ prices for American materials and sold their products in America for _____ prices.
4. Colonists in New England bought _____ from the West Indies and made it into _____. Because of high British taxes, some colonists became _____.
5. The _____ and _____ War ended in 1763. _____ was victorious.

Who or what were the following:

1. Nathaniel Bacon
2. General Braddock
3. John Peter Zenger
4. Parliament
5. Watertown

CHAPTER 3

Revolution and Independence

DIFFERENCES BETWEEN ENGLAND AND THE COLONIES GREW BITTER

The French and Indian War ended in 1763. England now had a big empire in America and India. But the wars against France had been costly. And the new territories would be expensive to govern. Many British soldiers would be needed in America to keep peace with the Indians. England thought that the colonists should be taxed to help pay these added expenses.

In order to stay out of trouble with the Indians, England forbade settlers to move beyond the mountains in the western part of the colonies. Thus the British would need fewer troops. This rule angered fur traders and small farmers who wanted to move farther west. It also upset businessmen who expected to get rich quickly by buying up western lands at a low price.

The Colonists Resisted New British Taxes

England began to collect more taxes on American trade in order to pay for British officials and soldiers in America. In addition, the English started to enforce the tax laws more strictly. For example, the colonists had seldom paid the import tax on molasses, and the British had not tried hard to collect it. In 1764 this tax was reduced, but the British began to enforce the law.

Next, the colonists were ordered to buy tax stamps. These stamps were to be put on all documents, advertisements, ship clearance papers and newspapers. With the money raised in this way, England intended to pay the wages of British soldiers in America and the salaries of some of her colonial officials.

This angered the colonists. Regulating trade for the good of the British Empire was one thing. Putting taxes on trade in order to raise money for the king's officials in America was something else. Until then the colonists had often put pressure on British officials by threatening to withhold their pay. That is one way in which voters can make sure that their government works for them. The colonists wanted the right to say how money would be raised and how it should be spent. The Stamp Act would give them no voice in such matters. So the colonists sent representatives to a Stamp Act Congress in New York. The congress agreed that colonists should pay only those taxes that they voted for themselves. This idea became the well-known slogan, "no taxation without representation."

American colonists refused to buy and use tax stamps. Many American merchants stopped trading with England. Because of this, Parliament was finally forced to repeal the Stamp Act.

But the colonists continued to disobey British regulations on trade. Often they did not raise enough money to pay for British troops in the colonies.

The Townshend Acts Were Very Unpopular

In 1767 England's new minister, Charles Townshend, decided to clear up this situation. He had Parliament pass new laws to tighten British government in the colonies. First, there were to be taxes on the paint, paper, glass and tea bought abroad by the colonists. This money would be used to pay royal governors and other British officials in America. Next, there were to be more customs officers and soldiers in America to enforce trade regulations. And special English courts were to be set up in America to try smugglers. The colonial assembly in New York was abolished because it refused to raise money to pay the British soldiers in that colony.

The colonists felt that the Townshend Acts were worse than the Stamp Act. These acts meant that there would be more taxation without representation. Besides, if Parliament could abolish the New York Assembly, it could abolish other colonial assemblies. Then Americans would have no self-government at all. The Massachusetts Assembly spoke out strongly against the new acts and called on the other colonies to do the same. Once again American merchants stopped buying British goods.

Meanwhile, British officials began to search American homes and stores for smuggled goods. To help enforce the Townshend Acts, more British troops arrived in the American seaports. These troops were, of course, very unpopular among the colonists.

Once, in March 1770, some British soldiers and Bostonians got into a scuffle. Five colonists were killed. Hotheaded colonists like Samuel Adams called this a "massacre," but an American jury freed the British soldiers.

Finally, there was so much opposition in the colonies that Parliament repealed the Townshend Acts—all but the tax on tea. The king's ministers said they would no longer try to raise money in America with taxes voted by Parliament.

Many colonial merchants now wanted to let well enough alone. Other Americans, such as Samuel Adams in Massachusetts, urged that people continue to oppose England. After all, Adams and his friends pointed out, the old trading regulations were still on the books. England was using customs officers, soldiers and the navy in order to catch smugglers. And the English government had never backed down on its right to tax the colonists.

Then the British government caused the disputes to start all over again. In 1773, they let the East India Tea Company ship tea directly to America and sell it there cheaply. This would help the company to get rid of an over-supply of tea. At the same time, it would allow the Americans to buy tea at a low price. However, Americans saw this issue differently. They claimed that it would take the tea business away from American merchants, and it would make Americans pay the tax on tea. The Americans opposed this tax on principle.

American merchants refused to let the tea ships unload. In Boston, anti-British "patriots" went on board the tea company's ships and dumped the tea into the water. Some Americans thought this was going too far. The British government decided to punish Boston, and Parliament passed laws to do this.

The port of Boston was closed. No ships were allowed to enter or leave the harbor. No longer could the people of Massachusetts elect their own assembly. It would be appointed. Another law said that because colonial juries were too soft, certain prisoners could be tried in England instead of in the colonies. A British general was made Governor in Boston.

The First Continental Congress Met in 1774

Americans called these acts "intolerable." If Parliament could make such rules for Boston and Massachusetts, it could do the same thing in any other colony. The Americans must do something. In 1774 the colonies sent representatives to a meeting in Philadelphia. This meeting was known as the First Continental Congress.

The Continental Congress stated that all of the colonies opposed the Intolerable Acts. Congress urged the colonists to organize local militia and start military training. They also planned to have Americans stop buying British goods. Then they agreed to meet again a year later.

THE WAR OF INDEPENDENCE BEGAN IN 1775

By the spring of 1775, colonists in the Boston area were gathering arms and training soldiers. The port of Boston was still closed and the city was occupied by British troops. General Gage, the British commander in Boston, learned that colonists had gathered guns in the town of Concord. He sent troops to Concord to seize the guns.

The colonists had been expecting this move. As soon as British troops left Boston, William Dawes and Paul Revere rode through the countryside to warn everybody. On the morning of April 19, 1775, British troops met a few colonial soldiers on the village green in Lexington. The British troops fired at them and went on to Concord. There they fired on local soldiers and captured the hidden guns. Then they turned back to Boston. But on the way, Americans fought them from behind trees and stone walls. By the time the British reached Boston, they had lost more than 250 men. About 100 Americans had been killed. War had begun.

George Washington Was Given Command of the American Forces

Three weeks later the Second Continental Congress met in Philadelphia and took charge of the war. They chose George Washington, a Virginia delegate at the Congress, to fill the position of commander-in-chief of the new Colonial Army.

Before Washington reached Massachusetts, Americans occupied Breeds Hill and Bunker Hill across the river from Boston. British troops drove the Americans away, but they lost many men. Farther west, Ethan Allen and a few soldiers, called the Green Mountain Boys, captured Fort Ticonderoga in northern New York.

All summer long companies of volunteers from other colonies joined Washington outside of Boston. Here Washington drilled the troops. Then he sent General Knox to bring cannons from Fort Ticonderoga across the mountains. When the cannons arrived in March of 1776, Washington placed them on high ground so they could be fired into Boston. When he saw the cannons, the British general left the city with his army. Boston was free from British rule.

The Second Continental Congress Chose Independence

Meanwhile, the Second Continental Congress sent a petition to the King of England. It asked the king to stop using armies against the colonies but the king declared that the colonists were rebels. He hired Hessian soldiers from Germany to fight in America. The colonists saw that they either had to give up completely or keep on fighting. Gradually all of the congressional delegates agreed that that they would have to make a clean break with England.

In June of 1776, it was proposed in Congress that "these United Colonies are, and of a right ought to be, free and independent states." One month later, the motion was adopted. *The Declaration of Independence* was published on July 4.

The Declaration was drawn up by a committee headed by Thomas Jefferson. It explained the theory of government in which the delegates believed. All men, it said, are born with an equal right to life, liberty and the pursuit of happiness. If a government disregards these rights, the people can rebel and form a new government. The Declaration then listed all the acts of the king and Parliament that the colonists thought were wrong. Since the king would not correct these wrongs, the colonists declared themselves free of English rule. As President of the Congress, John Hancock signed the Declaration first.

The colonies had declared that they were independent. They still had to prove it.

THE AMERICANS WON THEIR INDEPENDENCE

When the British troops left Boston, fighting came to an end in New England. Meanwhile, however, a new and bigger British army took over New York City. General Washington was unable to defend the city. He kept his army in New Jersey and Pennsylvania. Then, in a surprise move on December 26, 1776, Washington and his troops crossed the Delaware River at Trenton. There they captured supplies and a large number of Hessian troops. A few days later they defeated some British troops at Princeton and took more guns. But in New York City, the British were secure.

The British Suffered a Costly Defeat at Saratoga

The next year, 1777, British generals planned a campaign to split the colonies in two. One British army would march south from Canada toward New York City. Another army would march north from New York City. They would meet in Albany and cut off New England from the other colonies. It was a good plan. That summer General Burgoyne's army from Canada reached the Hudson River valley. But General Howe in New York took his troops to Philadelphia and captured that city instead! This left General Burgoyne's army to fight alone far away from his supplies. Near Saratoga, New York, American armies fought and won two important battles. Burgoyne's whole army had to surrender.

Saratoga was the first big American victory and it gave the

colonists new courage. As a result of this victory, Benjamin Franklin was able to persuade the French to help the colonists. France declared war on England. The King of France promised to send money and soldiers to America.

Before help from France arrived, Washington's army spent a cold and hungry winter at Valley Forge. In nearby Philadelphia the British were warm and well fed. The next spring, a new British general arrived in Philadelphia. He took his army back to New York and stayed there for the rest of the war. Philadelphia was left in American hands.

During this period of the war, an American spy named Nathan Hale was captured by the British and put to death. Another American, General Benedict Arnold, turned traitor and went over to the British side.

The Battle of Yorktown Ended the War

The British had failed to win the war in New York, Boston or Philadelphia. So they tried to win it in the South. A British army under General Cornwallis took Savannah, Georgia, and Charleston, South Carolina. Then the British marched northward. They hoped that many colonists would join their side, but not many did. American soldiers under General Nathaniel Greene were outnumbered, but they fought, retreated, and fought again. In Virginia, other American troops commanded by a French officer, the Marquis de Lafayette, also made repeated attacks on the British. Finally, Cornwallis marched to Yorktown on the Virginia coast to get fresh supplies by sea.

By now a French fleet was in the Atlantic Ocean and a new French army had joined General Washington. French ships defeated a British fleet off the coast of Virginia and drove it away. This left Cornwallis and his army alone in Yorktown. Then General Washington marched his American and French soldiers from New York to Virginia. Yorktown was surrounded. General Cornwallis and the British army

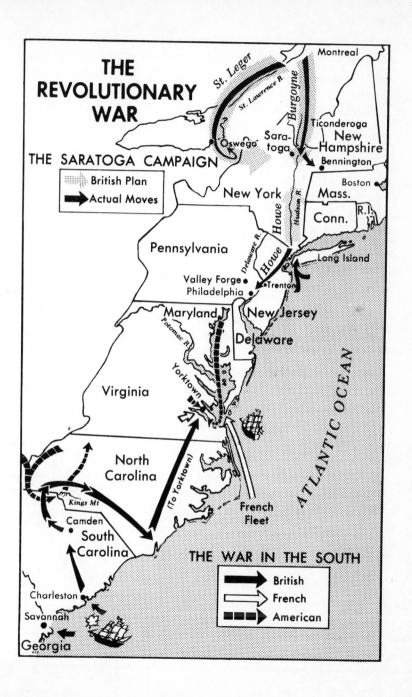

THE REVOLUTIONARY WAR

THE SARATOGA CAMPAIGN

British Plan
Actual Moves

THE WAR IN THE SOUTH

British
French
American

St. Leger
St. Lawrence R.
Montreal
Burgoyne
Oswego
Ticonderoga
New Hampshire
Sara-toga
Bennington
Boston
New York
Mass.
Hudson R.
Howe
Conn.
R. I.
Pennsylvania
Delaware R.
Howe
Long Island
Valley Forge
Trenton
Philadelphia
New Jersey
Maryland
Delaware
Potomac R.
Yorktown
Virginia
(To Yorktown)
North Carolina
Kings Mt.
French Fleet
Camden
South Carolina
ATLANTIC OCEAN
Charleston
Savannah
Georgia

were forced to surrender to Washington on October 19, 1781.

Yorktown was the last battle to be fought in America. Two years later a peace treaty was signed, and British armies left New York. England agreed that the colonies were now free and independent. The colonies could have all the land west to the Mississippi River. The War for Independence was over.

INDEPENDENCE BROUGHT CHANGES IN AMERICAN LIFE AND GOVERNMENT

After they declared their independence, the Americans had to organize new governments. In doing so, they changed what they thought was wrong with the colonial governments. The new state governments were made more democratic.

Men remembered the strong royal governors who had stood in the way of colonial assemblies. So they did not give the new state governors too much power. They did not trust governors, even though the new ones were to be elected by the state assemblies or by the people. State assemblies were given more power. In most states, more people were given the right to vote. And the western counties were better represented in the new governments.

The new state governments were based on the idea of *separation of powers*. Most colonists believed that there should be three branches of government. A legislative branch —the assembly—would make laws. An executive branch— the governor—would enforce the laws. A judicial branch —the courts—would interpret the laws. Power would be divided among all three branches. Colonists made the legislative branch the strongest of the three. Usually the legislature was made up of two houses. It did more than make laws. In most states, the legislature elected a governor and appointed the judges.

The new state legislatures passed laws that made people

more nearly equal. They broke up many large estates that were owned by British subjects. This land was then sold in small lots to Americans. State legislatures took over land owned by the king or proprietors and sold it to small farmers. They repealed laws that said a man must leave all of his land to his oldest son. And they ended most of the ties between church and state. Such laws tended to break down special privileges and promote equality.

Similar changes took place outside the law. Not all colonists wanted independence. During the war about one-third of them had sided with England. These people included some of America's oldest and richest families. "Rebels" made their lives miserable. After the rebels won the war, the Tories, as these people were called, lost their influence and importance. Some of them were forced to give up their property, and many of them had to leave the colonies. Many Tories wanted to leave because they did not approve of the kind of democracy that the colonists set up.

The New National Government Was Weak

Making the national government democratic was a harder task than organizing new state governments. Nobody wanted a strong government. All during the war the Second Continental Congress had been the entire national government. Although the Congress had no legal power, it ran the country. It had taken charge of the war, declared independence, built an army and navy, made treaties with France and the Indians and printed paper money. The members of Congress knew there should be a legal government. Their plan for a central government of the united colonies was discussed while the war went on. It was called the Articles of Confederation. All thirteen states finally accepted this plan in 1781.

The Articles of Confederation provided for a Congress that was to be elected by the state legislatures. But this

Congress could not collect any taxes or make trade laws. There was no "executive," such as a governor or president. All work would be done by congressional committees. It was not a strong government, but it lasted until after the war had ended.

REVIEW ACTIVITIES

1. Why did England tax the colonists more heavily after the French and Indian War? Why did the colonists object?
2. What were the Townshend Acts? Why were they passed?
3. What four things did the First Continental Congress do?
4. Why was the Battle at Saratoga so important?
5. How did the new state governments differ from the colonial governments?

Select the words that best complete the following sentences. (*Please do not write in this book.*)

1. The commander of all Colonial armies was _____ _____. He was appointed by the _____ _____.
2. The English king hired _____ soldiers from _____ to fight in America.
3. The Declaration of Independence says all men are born with an equal right to "_____, _____ and the pursuit of happiness."
4. The new state governments were based on the idea of _____ of _____.
5. The Second _____ Congress was the entire American government until _____.

Who or what were the following:

1. The Stamp Act
2. East India Tea Company
3. John Hancock
4. General Cornwallis
5. Tories

CHAPTER 4

Confederation and Constitution

THE ARTICLES OF CONFEDERATION HAD SEVERAL DRAWBACKS

The Articles of Confederation were accepted in 1781, two years before the war with England came to an end. So when the war was over, the new United States had a national government to sign a peace treaty. But at that time the United States was hardly a nation at all. It was a league of separate and independent states. That is why it was called a "confederation."

The federal, or national, government was like the Second Continental Congress. Members of Congress were appointed by state assemblies. Each state had only one vote in Congress, and two-thirds of the states had to agree before a new law could be passed. There was no governor or president, nor were there any judges. The national government consisted only of Congress.

Under the Articles of Confederation, the new government

really had very little power. Congress could not levy taxes. If it needed money, Congress had to ask the states to contribute. It did not have power to regulate trade. All it was expected to do was make treaties, send ambassadors to other nations, declare war or arrange for peace. Congress could determine what money should be worth, but it could not coin money. And Congress could run a federal post office system. That was about all it could do. Everything else was done by the states. Each state levied its own taxes, regulated its own trade, raised its own army and coined its own money. The states were supposed to handle their own problems.

But for all its weaknesses, the government under the Articles of Confederation did make one wise decision. This decision concerned the country's western lands. In Chapter 6 we shall read about the land decision.

THE NEW NATION FACED MANY PROBLEMS

After the war the worst problems facing the new nation had to do with money and business. In colonial times, Americans bought and sold mostly with England. When the war was over, England treated American businessmen as foreigners and refused to buy certain produce from them. England also insisted that most of her trade be carried on English ships. American shippers and fishermen had to find new ways of making money, and that took time. Without profit from foreign trade, there was not enough cash for use at home.

During the war, American factories had been set up to supply the necessary clothing and tools. After the war, British clothing and tools could be bought at lower prices than those made in America. American factories were free to produce anything they wanted, but many could not make a profit. Money was scarce. Farmers could not get cash for their products. They could not pay their taxes, and they were unable to pay off their debts. When state courts ordered them to pay their debts, angry farmers stopped the judges from meeting. Farmers led by Daniel Shays even tried to seize the guns that were stored in Springfield, Massachusetts. The farmers had to be dispersed by state soldiers. Seven new states tried to help by printing paper money. But the new paper bills were merely promises, and merchants would not use them.

Conditions improved gradually, but only because merchants and shippers found new markets. It took time for American business to adjust to the conditions that followed the war. And the states could do very little to help. Some men began to think that a strong central government might be able to do more. Certainly, they said, a strong central government was necessary to deal with many of the problems that confronted the country.

England continued to bar American traders from many markets in the British Empire. American shipowners received no help from the government when they sought new markets. England would not sign any trade agreement with her former colony. English soldiers remained in western forts, and Congress could not get them to leave. Spain controlled the mouth of the Mississippi River, and Congress could not get Spain to let American farmers ship their goods past New Orleans. States began to quarrel among themselves. They charged taxes, or tariffs, on goods that were sent from one state to another. This was bad for trade. New York State even put a tax on goods that passed through it from Connecticut to New Jersey. States also argued over fishing rights in Chesapeake Bay.

THE CONSTITUTIONAL CONVENTION MET TO STRENGTHEN THE NATIONAL GOVERNMENT

The conditions just described convinced many men that more power should be given to the federal government. It was proposed that a convention meet in Philadelphia in May of 1787 to change the Articles of Confederation. Congress issued invitations to all the states. The delegates chosen by the states were all important men in their states. George Washington was appointed Chairman of the Constitutional Convention. Benjamin Franklin was there. He was an old man now, but his mind was as keen as ever. Many of the delegates, on the other hand, were young men. Alexander Hamilton of New York was only thirty. Hamilton favored strong power for the central government. James Madison of Virginia, who was but a few years older than Hamilton, had helped to write his state's constitution. Since Madison probably worked harder than any other delegate, some historians call him the "Father of the Constitution."

Most of the convention delegates were men of wealth and social position. Although they had been rebels themselves, they did not approve of uprisings such as Daniel Shays's rebellion in Massachusetts. They did not want to give power to the mass of the people, and some of them feared mob rule. The delegates met from May until September of 1787. Altogether, there were fifty-five delegates, but seldom were there more than thirty present at one time. In the beginning, the delegates planned to change the Articles of Confederation. But many delegates believed that the Articles should be done away with entirely and replaced by a new form of government. They wanted a government that would be strong enough to defend American interests abroad, pay off the war debts, protect property rights and put down rebellions such as Shays'.

For such powers the government would need money. Therefore, the new national government would have to levy its own taxes. Such a government would require the power to make laws concerning trade between the states, as well as trade with foreign countries. It would need power, too, to enforce its own laws.

The convention delegates agreed that these important new powers should be added to the power that the national government already had. They also agreed upon the kind of government they wanted. It would be a government of *checks and balances* with three separate branches. It would be very similar to the governments that existed in the thirteen states. There would be a congress to make laws. An executive, a president, would enforce these laws. A system of courts would interpret the laws.

The big questions were: Should the national government be an agent of the people, or an agent of the states? Should Congress represent the people directly, or should it represent the states?

It was decided that Congress would consist of two houses. One house, the Senate, would represent the states. Each state assembly would choose two senators to represent it. The members of the second house, the House of Representatives, would be elected by the people. Population would determine the number of representatives that each state would elect. In other words, the larger states would have more representatives than the smaller states. The larger states had more power in the House of Representatives, but the smaller states could protect their interests in the Senate.

The President would be chosen by a special group known as the *Electoral College*. The total number of representatives and senators in each state would determine how many men that state could elect to this college. The Electoral College would then elect a President. Judges were to be appointed by the President and approved by the Senate.

By September of 1787 the new Constitution was completed. The next step was to have it approved by the states. A special convention would be held in each state to vote on the new form of government. When nine states approved, the new government would go into effect.

Some People Opposed the Constitution

Not everyone favored the new Constitution. Voters were divided into two groups. Federalists, men with property, businessmen, lawyers and owners of large southern plantations favored the Constitution. Anti-Federalists, mostly trademen and small farmers, felt that the new government would have too much power. They were afraid it would be like the strong British government they had suffered under as colonists. They thought any strong government was a mistake. They said that "the little man" could not be sure that the new government would not hurt him.

It was doubtful that the Constitution would be accepted. Then the Federalists promised that they would help add a list of rights to the Constitution. The new government would not be able to take these rights away. People called this statement of rights a *Bill of Rights*. These rights were guaranteed later by the first ten changes, or amendments, to the Constitution. When this promise was made, many Anti-Federalists agreed to vote for the Constitution. Eleven states approved it. Anti-Federalists in North Carolina and Rhode Island held out longer. But in 1789 the Constitution went into effect.

THE NEW GOVERNMENT HAD WIDE POWERS

The Constitution provided for a strong national government of checks and balances. It differed from the Articles of Confederation in a number of ways. First, as we have already seen, the *form* of central government was different. There would be a legislature composed of two houses, an executive and a system of courts.

Second, the new national government would have more powers than the old one had. Under the Confederation, Congress could make treaties, declare war, make peace, run a postal system and decide on the value of the money.

Under the Constitution, the national government was given these powers and many more. Now Congress could pass rules to regulate trade between the states and trade with foreign nations. Congress could coin money and control its value. It could say how foreigners could become citizens. It could make national laws about bankruptcy—that is, about men who could not pay their debts. At the same time, each state had to give up its right to do any of these things.

An important new power gave Congress the right to raise money through taxes or by borrowing. Now Congress could tax the people directly and put taxes on imports. Congress could pay all national officials without having to ask the states for money.

Another source of strength for the federal government was that the Constitution was declared the supreme law of the land. Not only did the states surrender certain rights to the federal government, but they also agreed that no state would pass a law that would contradict the Constitution. State officials were required to uphold the Constitution, and state judges were obliged to enforce the Constitution in state courts. Furthermore, the Constitution provided for a national system of courts to uphold the federal law.

The Constitution Provided for a System of Checks and Balances

There are, however, limits to the power of the national government. The Constitution provides that the national government has only those powers that are given to it and no more. Congress may not pass laws for which the Constitution does not give it power. All laws passed by Congress, as well as by the states, must be in keeping with the Constitution.

The new form of government also provided that no one branch could act entirely without the approval of another branch. For instance, the men who wrote the Constitution made sure that Congress had a check on the President. The President was empowered to enforce the laws of Congress, command the armed forces, carry on foreign affairs and make treaties. But every important official appointed by the President had to be approved by the Senate. Every treaty the President made had to be approved by two-thirds of the Senate before it could go into effect. Although the President would command the armed forces, Congress would vote the money for them and indicate how the money would be spent. Congress was given the right to remove a president from office by a process known as *impeachment*. Thus, if the House of Representatives believed that the President was guilty of breaking a law, it could bring charges against him. If two-thirds of the Senate decided that he was guilty, the President would be removed from office. Impeachment proceedings have been undertaken against only one President, Andrew Johnson. The vote in the Senate was one short of two-thirds, so he was not removed from office.

The power of Congress was held in check also. No act of Congress would become law until the President had agreed to it. The President could refuse to sign an act, and he could *veto* an act of Congress. If he did so, Congress could pass the law only if two-thirds of the senators and representatives agreed that it should be passed. When legal cases arose over laws that Congress had passed, the courts would decide if the laws were in keeping with the Constitution.

Congress is a check on the President. The President is a check on Congress. And, to be sure that all acts of the President and Congress are constitutional, the courts are a final check. A government that is set up in this way is called a government of checks and balances. This system can lead to delays and disputes among the branches, but it keeps one branch from becoming too powerful.

How would such a government work? That was the question that the new republic faced in 1789.

REVIEW ACTIVITIES

1. What problems did the nation face after the War for Independence?
2. What is a government of checks and balances?
3. How does our Constitution provide for a government of checks and balances?
4. Why did Anti-Federalists oppose the new Constitution?
5. What new powers were given to the central government under the Constitution?

Select the words that best complete the following sentences. (*Please do not write in this book.*)

1. _____ _____ was elected Chairman of the Constitutional Convention that met in _____.
2. Congress consists of two _____, the House of Representatives and the _____.
3. Under the _____, the President is chosen by the _____ _____.
4. The first _____ amendments to the Constitution are called the _____ of _____.
5. _____ can remove the President from office by a process known as _____.

Who or what were the following:

1. Constitutional Convention
2. Daniel Shays
3. Federalists
4. Anti-Federalists

CHAPTER 5

Federalists and Anti-Federalists

WASHINGTON WAS ELECTED OUR FIRST PRESIDENT

Members of the new Congress met in New York in February of 1789. When the votes for President were counted, they found that every man in the Electoral College had voted for George Washington. Washington had been a colonel in the French and Indian War, and he had commanded the Colonial Army during the War for Independence. He had been the Chairman of the Constitutional Convention in Philadelphia. Everybody wanted Washington to be the first President of the United States. He had often proved his courage and ability, even under discouraging conditions.

John Adams of Massachusetts was elected the first Vice-President. Adams had been a member of the Second Continental Congress, and he had worked on the peace treaty that ended the War for Independence. Under the Articles of Confederation, he was our minister to England.

The New Government Started to Work

The first problem of the new government was how to raise money to pay for its expenses. To do this, Congress put a tax, or tariff, on all imports into the United States. Another tax was placed on all ships that entered American ports.

Next, Congress passed laws that gave officers to President Washington to help him run the government. Congress created a Department of State to handle foreign affairs, a Treasury Department to handle money matters, and a War Department to handle national defense. A chief lawyer, or Attorney General, was appointed to handle legal matters. The Attorney General and the other heads of departments formed a group that later became the President's Cabinet.

Washington chose Thomas Jefferson as his Secretary of State. Jefferson, the author of the Declaration of Independence, was our minister to France under the Confederation. Jefferson was also an Anti-Federalist.

Hamilton's Financial Plan Was Adopted

Washington appointed Alexander Hamilton to head the Treasury Department. Hamilton was a strong Federalist who wanted the national government to improve conditions for business. What was good for trade and manufacture, he argued, was good for the nation. Hamilton believed that business needed confidence in the federal government and a sound money system.

Hamilton's plan was to pay off all war debts of the Continental Congress and the states. This would give businessmen confidence in the federal government. As a side effect, it would help speculators who had bought up old debt certificates at low prices. Anti-Federalists complained that this was unfair to the farmers and soldiers who had been paid in these certificates. Merchants had not accepted them at full value. Now the merchants would get full value from the government. Hamilton's plan also seemed unfair to the states, mostly southern, that had already paid off their debts. To satisfy the Southerners, Hamilton promised that the nation's capital would be established in the South. Congress then passed the laws that Hamilton wanted.

Congress also established the National Bank in 1791. The bank was owned partly by the government. It would issue paper money that businessmen could trust. It would also be a place to deposit federal funds. Jefferson and the Anti-Federalists opposed the National Bank. They claimed that the Constitution did not give Congress power to set up a bank. But Hamilton argued that Congress had power to do what was necessary for the good of the country. Congress agreed.

Jefferson Opposed Hamilton

Jefferson did not like many of Hamilton's laws. He thought that the national government was taking over too much power. Jefferson and his followers and Hamilton and his friends all believed in the Constitution. But they differed in their interpretation of it.

Jefferson did not want the federal government to do anything that was not specifically allowed by the Constitution. Federalists, on the other hand, believed that the government could do anything that was not specifically forbidden by the Constitution. Hamilton kept his eye on these words in the Constitution: "The Congress shall have power to . . . provide for . . . the general welfare of the United States." Federalists believed this gave Congress power to do almost anything that the senators and representatives thought would be good for the country. This is interpreting, or construing, the Constitution loosely. Those who think this way are sometimes referred to as "loose constructionists."

Jefferson kept his eye on the Tenth Amendment: "The powers not delegated to the United States by the Constitution

. . . are reserved to the states . . ." This exact interpretation is called "strict construction." Even today there is a difference of opinion as to which interpretation of the Constitution is correct.

Taxes Helped the Government Raise Money

In order to raise enough money to pay off old debts, Congress taxed certain goods that were made in the United States. This tax was called an *excise* tax. When the government put an excise tax on whiskey, many farmers objected. Since grain was too bulky to ship over mountain roads, farmers made whiskey from it. The whiskey tax cut into the farmers' profits. In Pennsylvania farmers started to rebel against the tax. President Washington called on four states to provide troops to stop the rebellion. The rebels were defeated and their leaders were captured.

The outcome of the *Whiskey Rebellion* proved that the new government could enforce its laws. It also made many farmers think that the Federalists who ran the government were not their friends.

By these acts, Washington's government put the new nation on a sound financial basis. But farmers and small tradesmen were unhappy with the methods used by the Federalists. Meanwhile, world events brought prosperity to American shippers and new problems to the American government.

WAR IN EUROPE BROUGHT PROBLEMS TO AMERICA

A revolution in France started in 1789. Four years later, the French had removed their king from the throne and had cut off his head. War began with England and it continued, off and on, for the next twenty years. The United States and France had a treaty of alliance. However, most of America's trade and shipping was with England, not with France. Therefore, if the United States joined France in a war against England, it would be bad for American businessmen.

President Washington wanted the United States to remain neutral. He said that the treaty of alliance between the United States and France did not apply. American shippers were free to trade with both sides during the war. So they started to carry goods from French colonies to Europe. Then England's navy began to stop American ships and to take off any French goods it found on board. The English also seized American goods that were bound for France. This cost American shippers a lot of money. The English even took British sailors off American ships and made them serve in the British Navy. Americans thought this was illegal.

The United States Signed Its First Two Treaties

President Washington sent Chief Justice John Jay to England in 1794 to obtain an agreement about shipping rights. Jay was also to obtain an agreement to have the English soldiers leave the forts in the American West. Although the soldiers were supposed to leave after the War for Independence, they had stayed on. Now they were causing trouble with the Indians.

Jay persuaded England to agree that British soldiers would leave the forts. But England was at war, and she could not afford to stop searching American ships. England agreed to pay for the American goods her navy took, but she refused to pay for French goods. Nor would she stop taking British sailors off American ships.

England also agreed not to prevent Americans from trading in the East Indies. She allowed so little trade with the West Indies, however, that the American Senate refused to accept that part of the treaty. Nobody was really satisfied with the Jay Treaty, but the Senate approved it. It was better to sign the treaty than to become involved in a war with England.

Although Jay's treaty was unpopular, it led to another

treaty that met with the approval of almost everybody. Spain had joined France in the war against England. Spain owned Louisiana and she was afraid that England might attack her colony. Since the Jay Treaty seemed to make America and England friends, Spain feared that the Americans might attack New Orleans. So in 1795 Spain signed a treaty with the American minister, Charles Pinckney. The Pinckney Treaty said that Americans could float goods down the Mississippi River and ship them out of New Orleans. This treaty pleased all western settlers.

PRESIDENT JOHN ADAMS HAD TROUBLE WITH FRANCE

President Washington had been re-elected in 1793. He served a second term of four years, but he would not agree to serve again. In 1797 John Adams, a Federalist, became the second President. The man with the second largest number of votes was Thomas Jefferson, an Anti-Federalist. He became the Vice-President.

The European war continued while Adams was the President. Since the Jay Treaty made it appear that America was friendly toward England, France started to seize American ships. America protested and President Adams sent three representatives to persuade the French to stop. The French minister would not even meet with the Americans. He demanded that they pay him a bribe first. So the Americans came home. When their story was made public, everyone was angry. Why should Americans pay a bribe? "Millions for defense," they said, "but not one cent for tribute." Congress voted money for a larger army and navy. American ships fought French ships. This was an unofficial kind of war. Many Federalists felt that America should declare war officially.

Most Anti-Federalists believed differently. France was now a republic like the United States. France stood for equality and democracy. Many small traders, workmen and farmers in America liked France better than England. Their newspapers attacked the Federalists and defended France. The possibility of war with France gave Federalists an excuse to clamp down on their critics. The Federalists claimed that their opponents were dangerous to the United States.

Congress passed two laws in 1798 to weaken the opposition. The Alien Act gave the President power to expel foreigners from the United States. The Sedition Act made it a crime to criticize the President or the government in word or in print. More than twenty newspaper editors were arrested for criticizing the government.

Jefferson and the Anti-Federalists said that the Alien and Sedition Acts were unconstitutional. Legislatures in Virginia and Kentucky passed resolutions declaring that these laws had no force.

President Adams did not like criticism, but he knew that war would be bad for the country. In 1800, when a new government came to power in France, America and France signed a treaty. France agreed that goods on American vessels would not be seized. For the moment, this treaty ended the danger of war with France. It also made Adams unpopular with his Federalist friends.

THE ANTI-FEDERALISTS ELECTED THE NEXT PRESIDENT

In the presidential election of 1800, the Federalists were defeated. Thomas Jefferson, the leading Anti-Federalist, was elected. Small farmers and tradesmen had increased in numbers. They did not like the excise tax, the National Bank and the Alien and Sedition Acts. They called themselves Democratic-Republicans and voted for Jefferson because he opposed all of these measures.

Actually, Jefferson almost lost the election. His running mate was Aaron Burr. Republican electors all voted for both

Jefferson and Burr, and the result was a tie. According to the Constitution, a tie was to be settled in the House of Representatives. In the House, many Federalist congressmen voted for Burr. Alexander Hamilton considered Jefferson the better man, and so he helped to see that Jefferson was elected. But the United States had almost elected as President the man who had been chosen Vice-President. To make sure this did not happen again, Congress passed the Twelfth Amendment. The states approved it in 1804. After that time, electors cast two votes—one for President and the other for Vice-President.

￼ While Adams was President, the Capitol building and the White House were built in the District of Columbia. The federal government moved from Philadelphia to Washington. Jefferson was the first President to be inaugurated in Washington.

Jefferson Reversed Several Federalist Policies

Leading Federalists thought that Jefferson was a dangerous radical. Today, however, his ideas do not seem very radical. In his first address to Congress, Jefferson said he was for a "wise and frugal government." He was for "honest friendship with all nations, entangling alliances with none." He would support "the state governments in all their rights." The most radical thing that Jefferson ever did was to receive foreign dignitaries while dressed in his bathrobe!

￼ Jefferson's policy was to cut down the importance of the national government. Jefferson and Albert Gallatin, his Secretary of the Treasury, reduced taxes. The excise tax, the cause of the Whiskey Rebellion, was canceled. Both the army and the navy were reduced in size. With the money saved in these ways, Gallatin began to pay off the national debt. The Alien and Sedition Acts expired and were not renewed.

Jefferson and his friends wanted to reduce the number

of Federalists working for the government. During the last days of Adams's presidency, Congress had enlarged the system of federal courts, and Adams had appointed many Federalists as new judges. After Jefferson became the President, Congress was controlled by the Democratic-Republicans. Congress then repealed the law that provided for more judges and would not vote money to pay the new Federalist judges.

One of these judges, named Marbury, asked the Supreme Court to compel the government to appoint him. He sued the Secretary of State, James Madison. The Federalist judges on the Supreme Court wanted to help Marbury. But Chief Justice Marshall decided that the original law that empowered the courts to act in this case was not in keeping with the Constitution. Marbury lost. The decision in the case of *Marbury* versus *Madison* is important. It was the first time that the Supreme Court declared a law unconstitutional.

Meanwhile, the new Congress passed another law to create additional federal courts. This time Jefferson appointed Democratic-Republicans or Anti-Federalists to fill all new government posts. By giving jobs to Democratic-Republicans, he strengthened his own party.

Federalists were not happy to see the nation filling up with farmers who would become followers of Jefferson. But as a whole, the country was prospering.

By 1804 Jefferson's party was more popular than ever. When he ran for a second term, Jefferson was elected by a big margin. His administration kept taxes and government expenses low. The European war, which had stopped briefly from 1801 to 1803, started again. American exports began to increase, and American shippers made big profits by trading with the countries at war. But both England and France began to seize American ships. Neither Jefferson nor President Madison, who followed him in 1809, could make the warring countries leave American ships alone.

America Tried to Protect Her Shipping

Beginning in 1806, England declared all of France "blockaded." Any ship trading with France or a French territory would be captured. France then declared England under blockade and began to seize all ships that traded with England. England issued Orders in Council stating that only ships that stopped in England first could trade with France. France replied by seizing the ship and cargo of any captain who *did* stop in England first.

There was no way Americans could trade with Europe without risking capture by either France or England. There seemed to be no way for Jefferson's government to protect American shippers against such risks. The United States could not support a strong navy. And Jefferson's policy of saving money had reduced the navy to very few ships. In spite of the dangers, American exports to England and Europe increased. Prices were so high that American merchants could afford to lose two out of three ships and still make a profit.

Jefferson Avoided War

This situation might have continued, but England began taking sailors off American merchant ships for her own navy. Then, in June of 1807, a British wa.ship fired on the *Chesapeake*, one of the few warships of the United States Navy, and took four sailors off the ship. This was an attack on America, and many Americans wanted to fight back. Even though Jefferson did not want war, his peaceful efforts failed.

First, Congress passed the Embargo Act in December of 1807. This act forbade any ship to leave an American port for a foreign country. If England could not get food from America, perhaps she would agree to respect American ships. But England did not change her mind. American trade abroad almost stopped. Farmers could not sell their produce. Shippers lost money. Sailors were out of work.

After two years, the Embargo Act was canceled. To replace it, Congress passed the Non-Intercourse Act. This act allowed American ships to trade with most countries, but not with France or England. The new act did not help very much.

MADISON BARGAINED WITH FRANCE AND ENGLAND

President Jefferson had now served two terms. In 1808 James Madison, Jefferson's Secretary of State, was elected President. Madison had helped write the Constitution.

President Madison also was unable to protect American shipping rights. While Madison was President, Congress tried another law. Americans were permitted to trade with anyone. If England would agree that American ships could trade as neutrals, then America would agree not to trade with France. And, if France would stop capturing American ships, then America would not trade with England.

Napoleon, the French Emperor, pretended to cancel his laws against American ships. Madison then ordered Americans to stop trading with England. But this did not help matters. England would not change her laws, and Napoleon continued to seize American ships anyway. Actually, France had seized many more American ships than England. However, England's navy continued to take sailors off American ships. Many Americans demanded an end to this situation. They talked of war.

The West Demanded War

It was not the shippers who wanted war. In spite of British actions, the American shippers were making money. The War for Independence was over, and many rich Americans liked to regard themselves as English. Besides, many wealthy Americans did not like the French brand of equality. The demand for war came from somewhere else. It came from the West.

REVIEW ACTIVITIES

1. What were some of the first acts of the new Congress?
2. How did Hamilton plan to pay the national and state war debts? Who opposed his plans? Why?
3. What actions of England during her war with France angered the Americans?
4. Why did Congress pass the Twelfth Amendment? What change did it make?
5. Why did Congress pass the Embargo Act in 1807? How successful was this act?

Select the words that best complete the following sentences. (*Please do not write in this book.*)

1. Hamilton's followers were called _____. Those who agreed with Jefferson were called _____.
2. A tax on certain goods that are made in the United States is called an _____ tax. When a tax of this type was placed on _____, the farmers rebelled.
3. Charles Pinkney's Treaty was signed with _____. It allowed American goods to be landed and shipped again at _____ _____.
4. In the case of Marbury versus _____, the Supreme Court declared a law of Congress _____.
5. The demand for war against England did not come from the _____. It came from the _____.

Who or what were the following:

1. John Jay
2. Alien and Sedition Laws
3. John Adams
4. Orders in Council
5. The *Chesapeake*

CHAPTER **6**

The West and the War of 1812

DISPUTES AROSE OVER WESTERN LANDS

After the War for Independence, many American soldiers and farmers moved west. For the next hundred years, native Americans and immigrants continued this westward movement. The first to go were the pioneers. These people were hunters and independent farmers. They did not think much of aristocratic landowners or rich bankers. They were men who wanted to be on their own. The pioneers believed in equality and democracy for all.

Even during the War for Independence, pioneer families had settled in Tennessee. Daniel Boone found a way over the mountains into the fresh lands of Kentucky. Captain George Rogers Clark led soldiers even farther west to capture British forts in the area that is now Indiana and Illinois.

If American rebels won the war, the United States would own this western land. But would it be owned by the nation as a whole? Or would it be divided among the states? Six of the former colonies claimed the land for themselves. Some of them claimed the same land. The states without land claims did not want to join the new nation unless the federal government owned the disputed land. Maryland would not sign the Articles of Confederation until it was agreed that the western lands belonged to all thirteen colonies together.

Congress Decided How Western Lands Would Be Governed

When peace came in 1783, Congress had dealt with the western lands. This was one matter that the government settled wisely under the Articles of Confederation. All land north of the Ohio River would be divided into townships and sections that would be offered for sale. A section was one square mile. Out of every thirty-six sections, one would be used to support schools.

Congress also decided how the new land north of the Ohio River was to be governed. At first it would be run by Congress. Then, when there were enough people in an area, these people could elect their own legislature. After the population had increased even more, the area could become a state. The new state would enter the Union as an equal partner with the first thirteen states. This law, passed in 1787, was called the Northwest Ordinance. All settlers were promised the right to a trial by jury. There was to be freedom of religion, and human slavery was forbidden. Under these conditions, settlers began to move into the Ohio Territory.

The first settlers found that Indians often caused them trouble. Indians hunted for their living and when farmers cut down trees, the Indians were no longer free to hunt. So they fought the settlers. The Indians were helped by fur traders and by British soldiers who still remained in many western forts. The Indians defeated two American forces that were sent to fight them. Then President Washington sent General Anthony Wayne into the Ohio Territory with a large army. Wayne defeated the Indians in a battle at Fallen Timbers in 1794. The Indians gave up most of Ohio to the settlers. Two years later British soldiers finally moved out of the forts in United States territory. After this, Ohio was a much safer place for settlers.

Meanwhile several thousand farmers and their families had moved into Kentucky and Tennessee. These men wanted to float their produce down the rivers to New Orleans. They were pleased, therefore, when Spain signed the Pinckney Treaty in 1795. This treaty gave them shipping rights in New Orleans.

The section of the Northwest Ordinance that provided for the admission of new states into the Union seemed like a good idea to the men who were writing the Constitution. As a result, they included a similar provision in it. In 1791 Vermont was admitted as the first new state. Soon pioneers who had moved west began to form new states. Kentucky became a state in 1792, and four years later Tennessee was admitted to the Union.

A new land law passed by Congress in 1800 made it easier for settlers to buy farms north of the Ohio River. Now a man could buy half a section—320 acres—at a cost of two dollars an acre. He was given four years to pay for his land. Many more settlers moved to Ohio and it became a state in 1803.

Western settlers were mostly independent farmers who were followers of Jefferson. Their state constitutions were very democratic and they permitted almost everyone to vote. This alarmed many Federalists who were conservative bankers, merchants and shippers. Federalists did not believe in such widespread democracy. They did not want to see the West grow so fast or become so large. They had little confidence in the common man.

Then, almost by accident, the West became much larger. This occurred while Thomas Jefferson was President. In 1799 Napoleon became head of the French government. Napoleon planned a big empire. He made Spain turn over the entire Louisiana Territory to France. This meant that France would control all trade at the mouth of the Mississippi. Jefferson was a friend of France, but he knew that France could now shut off American trade in New Orleans. If this happened, France would become an enemy of the United States.

Jefferson asked his minister in France to try to purchase land for the United States along one bank of the Mississippi. The American minister was unsuccessful. Then Napoleon's plans were changed. France and England were about to go to war again. Napoleon knew that he could never defend Louisiana against the English, so he decided to sell it. In 1803 he offered the whole territory to the United States for 15 million dollars. A treaty was signed. Jefferson was not sure that the Constitution gave the President power to purchase new land. However, the Senate approved the treaty.

United States territory now extended west to the Rocky Mountains. President Jefferson immediately sent Meriwether Lewis and William Clark to explore the new land. Lewis and Clark crossed the Rockies and traveled down the Columbia River to the Pacific Ocean. At that time the busy seaport of New Orleans already belonged to the Union. In 1812, the present state of Louisiana was admitted to the Union.

Indians and the English Caused Trouble for the Settlers

The rapid growth of the country made western settlers confident and proud. They looked forward to the day when farms would cover the entire continent. The Indians were all that stood in the way of their dream.

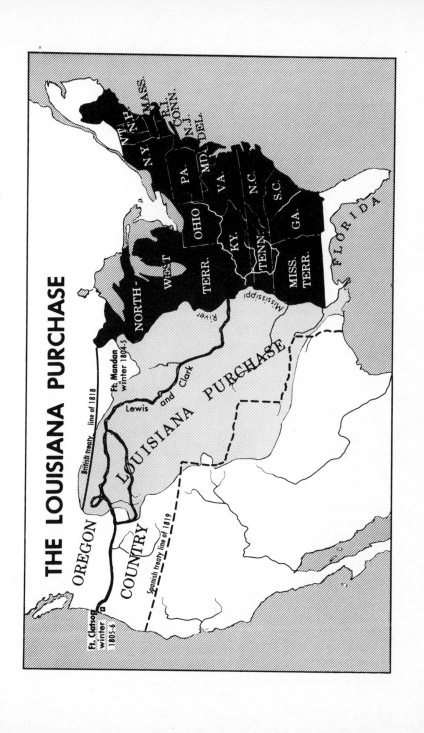

The story of the American Indian is a sad one. Indians lived in tribes, and most of their food was obtained by hunting. They could not live as the white men did and settle down to farming and business. That would change their whole way of life. To live their own way, the Indians needed hunting grounds. So they fought for them, and the settlers fought back.

After the Battle of Fallen Timbers in 1794, the Indians had to give ground. They were forced to give up land little by little. One of their leaders, Tecumseh, got some of the Indian tribes to stick together. These tribes had always fought each other. But now, said Tecumseh, they must unite to resist the white man. He did not want the Indians to fight the white man. He wanted them to stand together and refuse to surrender any more land.

When Tecumseh went south in 1811 to persuade other Indian tribes to join him, United States soldiers under General William Henry Harrison attacked the Indian village at Tippecanoe. After this attack, Indians disobeyed Tecumseh and raided settlements throughout Ohio and Indiana. They obtained guns from the English in Canada.

To western settlers it seemed as though the English in Canada were responsible for many Indian raids. That is why Americans in the new western states were against England. They talked of driving the English out of Canada. These Americans thought that it would be easy to conquer Canada.

AMERICA WENT TO WAR AGAINST ENGLAND

When Congress met in 1811, the big question was how to make England respect American shipping rights. The Embargo and Non-Intercourse Acts had failed. New representatives from the West with their eyes on Canada spoke out for war. Finally, after everything else had failed, President

Madison asked Congress to declare war against England.

The war began in June of 1812. Just two days before it started, England withdrew all of her acts against American shipping. But the Americans did not know about this for several weeks. The vote for war had been very close. Federalists, especially those in New England, had opposed war. Some Democratic-Republicans also believed that war would be a mistake. But the western states voted solidly for action.

The War Went Badly at the Start

Henry Clay of Kentucky, the new Speaker of the House, believed that the Americans could conquer Canada easily. However, the United States was not prepared for war. The regular United States Army had less than 10,000 soldiers and very few trained officers. State militia would not fight outside of their own states. And Congress had just defeated a bill that would have strengthened the navy.

Furthermore, the government had no money. The Embargo and Non-Intercourse Acts had reduced trade and cut down the income from tariffs. The National Bank, established by Hamilton in 1791, had been set up to last for twenty years. The government needed the National Bank to help borrow money, but in 1811 Congress voted not to continue it. The government then issued bonds. But bankers and merchants did not want war, and they bought few bonds.

The first campaigns of the war went badly for the United States. There were to be four drives into Canada. All of them failed. The British even captured Detroit in United States territory.

American Forces Began to Win Victories

By 1813 the American forces were larger and there were new commanders. Oliver Hazard Perry, a young naval officer, commanded a fleet of nine small ships on Lake Erie.

There he defeated a British squadron. "We have met the enemy," he reported, "and they are ours." American troops recaptured Detroit and crossed over into Canada. General Harrison's army beat the British and a force of 1200 Indians in Ontario. Tecumseh was killed in the battle. Other American troops captured York (now Toronto) and burned the government buildings. But the Americans did not occupy much of Canada.

When the British invaded the United States, they were stopped in northern New York. On Lake Champlain English ships were defeated by American ships under the command of Thomas Macdonough. But a larger English force landed in Maryland and easily marched on to Washington. There it burned down the new Capitol building and the White House before moving on to Baltimore. However, Baltimore held out and the British finally sailed away. While the British threatened the city, Francis Scott Key wrote the words of *The Star-Spangled Banner*, now our country's national anthem.

Meanwhile, the American navy fought well at sea, but it was too small to defeat the British. When the war began, the American navy barely had six warships of a decent size. The British, on the other hand, had about 240 warships that were as large or larger than ours. American warships put to sea, and they captured about 40 of England's merchant ships. When they met a British warship of equal size, they fought and won. But the large English navy stopped American shipping and kept our warships on the run.

In January of 1815 the biggest battle of the war was fought on land near New Orleans. A large English army had been sent to capture the city of New Orleans. Kentucky and Tennessee troops commanded by General Andrew Jackson had just defeated the Indians at Horseshoe Bend in Alabama. They marched on to defend Louisiana. Jackson's men fought from behind cotton bales, and the English were

badly beaten. However, the battle had no effect on the war.
A peace treaty had been signed two weeks earlier.

The Peace Treaty Changed Nothing

Early in the war, President Madison had appointed a
peace commission. The British had withdrawn their Orders
in Council that had hurt American shipping. It seemed possible that the war could end almost before it began. While
each side hoped for victory, the war went on.

Madison sent a peace commission including Henry Clay,
Albert Gallatin, and John Quincy Adams, the son of former
President Adams. These men persuaded England to agree
to a peace treaty that ended the war in December of 1814.

The treaty left things just as they had been before the war.
England had already withdrawn the rules that hurt American shipping. Nothing more was said about taking sailors
off American ships. And there was no mention of the British
in Canada who were helping the Indians. But everyone
was glad to end the war, and the Senate approved the treaty.

THE FEDERALISTS LOST POWER

One result of the war was that the importance of the Federalists in the United States came to an end. Federalists
had not wanted war in the first place, and many Federalist
leaders, especially those in New England, had opposed the
war after it started. They refused to buy government bonds
and they would not let the soldiers in their states fight.
They sold supplies to the British Navy and to the British
armies in Canada. The British were pleased, and they did
not stop merchant ships in Boston from going to sea.

Federalist delegates from New England met in Hartford
in 1814. They declared that Congress had no right to force
war upon a state that did not want it. They demanded
seven changes in the Constitution to protect the states from

the national government. The demands that the Federalists made and the way they had behaved during the war made them look foolish. As a political party, the Federalists were finished. The country was now united and at peace.

REVIEW ACTIVITIES

1. What did the Northwest Ordinance provide?
2. Why was it important for New Orleans to belong to the United States?
3. Who was Tecumseh? How did he try to protect the Indians? Why was he unsuccessful?
4. Why did the United States finally declare war on England in 1812?
5. What did the United States gain from the War of 1812?

Select the words that best complete the following sentences. (*Please do not write in this book.*)

1. The first new states to be admitted to the Union were _____ and _____.
2. President Jefferson sent _____ and _____ to explore land west of the Mississippi River.
3. The French Emperor _____ sold the _____ Territory to the United States for 15 million dollars.
4. Henry _____, Speaker of the House, boasted that Americans would conquer _____.
5. During the war _____ _____ from New England met in Hartford. They demanded states' rights and seven changes in the _____.

Who or what were the following:

1. Fallen Timbers
2. Tippecanoe
3. The National Bank
4. Oliver Hazard Perry
5. Andrew Jackson

CHAPTER 7

The Age of Jackson

AMERICA PROSPERED IN A PERIOD OF NATIONAL UNITY

The American War of 1812 was over in 1815. The long struggle in Europe against Napoleon ended that same summer. Then for forty years there were no big wars anywhere. The United States was free to grow and pay attention to internal problems. At first nearly everyone agreed about how the problems should be met. The followers of Jefferson even agreed with the Federalists.

The Democratic-Republicans Reversed Their Stand

Until 1816 the Jeffersonian Democratic-Republicans were against a strong central government. They feared it might be run by Federalists who would favor businessmen and be against the small farmer and the western settler. After the War of 1812, however, the Federalist Party was in disgrace. So the Democratic-Republicans were in control of the government. They began to let the federal government use those powers that they had voted against only a few years before.

Congress re-established the National Bank. Men who had talked against the Bank and said it was unconstitutional in 1811 voted for it in 1816. Paying for the war had been difficult without it. Even Jefferson's followers saw that the government needed the National Bank. Although they did not trust a bank run by Federalists, they thought that a bank run by Democratic-Republicans would be all right.

Congress also passed the kind of tariff law that Hamilton had wanted. During the embargo and the War of 1812, few manufactured goods were brought to America. Local businessmen set up factories to make the cloth and metal products that Americans needed. After the war, British merchants sold goods in the United States at low prices to force the new American factories out of business. American factory owners asked for protection. They wanted Congress to put a high tariff on imports so that British goods could not be sold so cheaply. Then Americans would buy American goods, and the new factories would make money.

Congressmen in the West and South had been against such a tariff before, because it would make them pay higher prices for manufactured goods. But in 1816 many of them voted for it. Henry Clay of Kentucky favored the tariff. Factories in the North and East, Clay said, would make goods to sell in the West. If American factories turned out enough goods, the United States would not have to worry about European shipping rights. This was part of what Clay called his *American System*.

New Routes Linked the East and the West

Roads and canals were needed in order to carry people and goods across the country. Many Westerners thought that the federal government should build these roads. They said that "internal improvements" such as roads, canals and harbors would make the country grow and that everybody would benefit from them. Congress was already building the Cumberland Road from Maryland into Ohio. Westerners wanted more such federal roads.

President Madison believed that such roads should be built by the states. He vetoed bills for roads and other internal improvements. But Madison's Secretary of State, James Monroe, became President in 1817. Monroe felt differently about internal improvements, and Congress spent national money for roads and harbors.

THE FEDERAL GOVERNMENT INCREASED ITS POWER

When it voted for a protective tariff, a national bank and internal improvements, Congress showed that it was ready to give strong powers to the federal government. The Supreme Court held the same point of view. Consider the argument over the National Bank. Strict constructionists said that Congress had no power to set up a national bank because it was not mentioned in the Constitution. The Supreme Court answered this argument. In the case of *McCulloch* versus *Maryland*, Chief Justice John Marshall and the Supreme Court decided that Congress had the "implied power" to set up a national bank. The Supreme Court, therefore, supported a "loose" construction of the Constitution.

The Supreme Court had also extended its own power. You will remember that in the case of *Marbury* versus *Madison* the Court had declared that an act of Congress was unconstitutional. In the case of *Fletcher* versus *Peck* in 1810, the Court declared a *state* law unconstitutional. Chief Justice Marshall built up the powers of the Supreme Court in other decisions as well.

The power of the national government was put to good use elsewhere. Questions left over after the War of 1812 were settled by diplomacy. The United States and England agreed on most of the line that now separates Canada and the United States. It would follow the St. Lawrence River, the Great Lakes and the 49th parallel to the Rocky Mountains. England and the United States agreed further that they would have no warships on the Great Lakes.

The United States added Spanish Florida to American territory in 1819. Before this, Indians often raided American farms and then ran across the border into Spanish Florida. Spain would not punish the Indians. During the War of 1812, Americans simply moved into western Florida and took it over. Then in 1818 an army under General Andrew Jackson marched into eastern Florida, defeated the Indians and captured two Spanish forts. At the same time Spain was having so much trouble with her other American colonies that she agreed to sell Florida to the United States. In return the United States promised not to claim the land that is now Texas.

The Monroe Doctrine Was Announced in 1823

Spain's other colonies in Latin America were in revolt. New states declared their independence and set up republican governments. There was a chance that other European powers might help Spain get back her colonies. And Russia was now claiming a part of the Oregon Territory. For neighbors, the United States preferred American republics to European colonies. But how could the United States keep European powers out of America?

Secretary of State John Quincy Adams was sure that the other European powers would not help Spain. He persuaded President Monroe to announce how the United States felt about European powers in America. In his message to Congress in 1823, President Monroe declared that no foreign state should try to put any more colonies in America. "The American continents," he said, "are henceforth not to be considered as subjects for future colonization by any European powers." He also made it clear that the United States would not interfere in European affairs. This statement is known as the *Monroe Doctrine.*

The United States was prosperous and at peace. No one opposed President Monroe. When it came time to elect a President in 1820, Monroe won every electoral vote but one. That vote was cast by a man who believed that George Washington should be the only President elected by every vote.

ANDREW JACKSON ALMOST WON THE PRESIDENCY IN 1824

The situation was different four years later. In 1824 three men wanted to be President. Andrew Jackson of Tennessee got the most votes in the Electoral College. John Quincy Adams was next. Henry Clay was a candidate, too. But no man had a majority. According to the Constitution it was up to the House of Representatives to choose the next President. Clay asked his friends to vote for Adams, and John Quincy Adams was elected. Jackson and his friends felt cheated. They claimed that Clay and Adams had joined in a corrupt bargain to steal the Presidency.

President Adams believed in broad use of federal power. He urged Congress to build roads and canals and to improve rivers and harbors. He hoped, too, that the government would promote agriculture, literature, science and art. But there was opposition to his administration. Jackson's friends still believed that their man should have been elected and they opposed the new President. In addition, Southerners generally opposed the broad use of federal power. Meanwhile, as the country grew, Jackson's friends became more numerous.

Robert Fulton had built the first profitable steamboat in 1807. By 1820 sixty steamboats on the western rivers carried farm produce to New Orleans and factory goods back to the farms. In New York State a canal was built from Lake Erie to the Hudson River. The Erie Canal, as it was called, was begun in 1817 and completed in 1825. After that, grain could be shipped cheaply from the West. In return, manufactured goods could be sent cheaply from the East. Now western farmers could make money in trade.

Meanwhile, American factories were producing more and more goods. Before the War of 1812, an inventor in Connecticut named Eli Whitney began to manufacture guns with "interchangeable parts." This speeded production and made repairs easier. Soon makers of all types of machines were copying Whitney's methods. This was the beginning of mass production in America. Cotton and woolen mills with power machinery started to operate in New England during the War of 1812. In time, other northeastern factories began to use machines to make such things as nails, bolts, hairpins and chains.

Eli Whitney also invented a machine called the cotton gin to take the seeds from raw cotton. This machine made cotton growing more profitable and cotton soon became more important to the South than tobacco. Cotton farmers moved west into what is now Alabama and Mississippi. There the population tripled within the next ten years. Mississippi became a state in 1817. Two years later Alabama joined the Union.

The Middle West grew just as rapidly. Between 1810 and 1820 the population of Ohio grew from 230,000 to 580,000. Ten years later it had reached 938,000. Indiana became a state in 1816, and Illinois joined the Union two years later. In 1820 Missouri and Maine became states.

In addition to grain, the mid-western states produced flour, meal, lard, salt pork, salt beef and fresh meat. These foods were shipped through the Erie Canal to eastern markets, and down the rivers to the South.

THE WEST HELPED ANDREW JACKSON WIN THE ELECTION OF 1828

In the new western states every man over twenty-one had the right to vote. In the original thirteen states, a man had to own land before he could vote. Most states changed that ruling soon after the Constitution was adopted, but they did require voters to pay a public tax. Then, because so many factory workers were moving west, even this requirement was dropped. By 1828 nearly every man over the age of twenty-one had the right to vote. In addition, he could now vote directly for an elector. At first, state legislatures usually had chosen the members of the Electoral College. But by 1828, every state but two had rules so that the voters could choose members of the Electoral College directly.

Before 1828 the average man often was not interested in politics. Now he was interested, and he could vote. Jackson was his hero. Many farmers were beginning to dislike the tariff. Others thought the National Bank was helping only the rich.

Jackson opposed the National Bank. He was also for keeping the Indians quiet and moving them farther west. In the election of 1828, Jackson won by a big margin. This marked the beginning of the Democratic Party as we know it today.

Jackson Wished to Help the Common Man

Andrew Jackson is one of the most famous American Presidents. He was a farm boy in western North Carolina during the War for Independence. He saw his father and

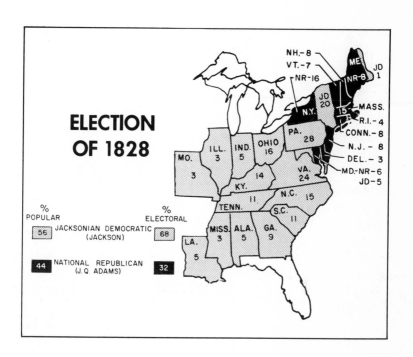

ELECTION OF 1828

NH.—8
VT.—7
NR-16
ME
NR-8
JD 1
JD 20
N.Y.
15 — MASS.
R.I.— 4
PA. 28
CONN.— 8
N.J. — 8
DEL.— 3
MD.-NR— 6
JD—5
MO. 3
ILL. 3
IND. 5
OHIO 16
VA. 24
KY. 14
N.C. 15
TENN. 11
S.C. 11
MISS. 3
ALA. 5
GA. 9
LA. 5

%
POPULAR

56 JACKSONIAN DEMOCRATIC
(JACKSON)

%
ELECTORAL

68

44 NATIONAL REPUBLICAN
(J.Q ADAMS)

32

brothers fight the British. He moved to Nashville and became a lawyer. He was the first member of the House of Representatives from Tennessee. He was a general who had fought the Indians, and he had won the only big battle of the War of 1812. Later, he was a senator. He did not believe that the national government had too much power. He said that its power should be used to help the people.

One way to have a government serve the people is to put friends of the people in office. Jackson appointed to office many men who had worked for his election. This was good politics. It kept his friends organized and eager to see that his party would be re-elected. It was a way to reward political supporters. Because of the saying "to the victors belong the spoils," he is said to have begun the *Spoils System.*

Jackson also believed that another way to help the people was to have the states handle their own problems. When the Supreme Court said that Georgia must permit the Indians to remain in that state, Jackson did not enforce the decision and he let Georgia handle the Indian problem in its own way. When Congress voted to build a national road in Kentucky, Jackson said such local roads should be built by the states themselves.

Jackson wanted the states to have more to say about banking and money. He did not believe that the federal government should have a national bank. His Secretary of the Treasury took federal money out of the National Bank and put it in state banks. When the National Bank's charter ran out, he said, it should not be renewed. According to Jackson, banking should be done locally to help the people.

But the big question during President Jackson's two terms in office was the tariff.

A Big Question About States' Rights Arose

In 1816 many congressmen from the South had voted for the tariff. A few years later they changed their minds, for

Congress had raised the tariff two or three times. This high tariff helped factories in the North and East, but it made farmers in the South pay high prices for the manufactured goods they needed. By 1828 the South was solidly against the high tariff.

A law in 1828 made the tariff so high that South Carolina objected. But Congress did not lower the tariff. By 1832 the people of South Carolina were very angry. The state legislature declared that South Carolina would not pay the tariff. The legislature would not let any federal officers collect it. If the federal government tried to collect the tariff in South Carolina, they said, the state would leave the Union.

This was a big question. Could one state "nullify" an act of Congress within its borders? Could one state refuse to obey an act of Congress? Could a state withdraw from the Union? In Congress, Senator Robert Hayne of South Carolina answered "yes" to these questions.

Once, when eastern senators tried to slow down the sale of western lands and western senators objected, Hayne rose to speak for them. Hayne was thinking about the tariff. He said western and southern states did not have to do everything that Congress ordered. Hayne said that the states could refuse. And, if they wanted to, they could even leave the Union.

Senator Daniel Webster replied that the nation was a union of people, not a union of states. The people, said Webster, could not let a state break up the Union. The Webster-Hayne debate is famous. It did not settle anything, but it set forth clearly the argument between the states and the federal government.

If South Carolina tried to nullify the national tariff law, which side would President Jackson take? He made it clear that he was for the Union. He asked Congress for power to use the armed forces in order to collect the tariff in South Carolina. But sober men did not want to let things go so far.

Led by Henry Clay, they agreed to a new tariff law in 1833. By this compromise, the tariff would be reduced a little each year. South Carolina decided not to try to nullify the tariff law. However, the state did not give up the right to do so. The big question of whether or not a state could nullify a federal law remained unanswered.

When Jackson's second term ran out, his party chose Vice-President Martin Van Buren from New York as its candidate. The people who were against President Jackson called themselves Whigs. They wanted Henry Clay to be elected. The Whigs favored the National Bank, more internal improvements, and a high tariff. But President Jackson and his party were popular and the country was prosperous. Their candidate, Martin Van Buren, was elected.

THE PANIC OF 1837 HURT THE COUNTRY

During Van Buren's presidency, the nation suffered a depression. It came so suddenly, it was called the Panic of 1837. Ever since 1820 the country had been prosperous. People had invested money recklessly in roads and canals. Many of the canals did not pay. People bought western land on credit. Expecting that prices would go way up, banks lent them money. When prices did go up, banks lent even more money.

A year before the Panic of 1837 began, President Jackson had tried to stop the buying of land on credit. In 1836 he ordered the Land Office to accept only hard cash in payment for public land. People who had deposited money in banks went to the banks to get gold or silver coins in order to make their payments. The banks did not have enough hard cash on hand to meet these demands. People lost confidence in banks and tried to withdraw all of their savings. But the banks had lent the money, and they could not get it back fast enough. Many of the loans were based on hopes for a rise in land prices. When the banks could not collect all the money that was owed to them, they had to go out of business.

When the banks failed, everybody suffered. Depositors lost their savings. People could no longer buy the things they needed. Factories had to cut wages or lay off workers. This meant there was even less money for people to spend. The federal government lost much of the money it had put into state banks.

On top of this, the price of cotton fell to less than half of what it had been. And what was worse, there was a crop failure in grain. Cotton planters could not sell at a profit. Wheat farmers had no wheat to sell. It was six years before business picked up again and returned to normal. President Van Buren's party did not want another national bank, but the government could not afford to lose money in shaky banks. After 1840, federal funds were kept in an "independent treasury." But this did not help the country to recover.

Meanwhile, there was another national election in 1840. This time the Jacksonian Democrats were defeated and the Whigs won the election.

WILLIAM HENRY HARRISON BECAME THE FIRST WHIG PRESIDENT

Candidates for the two political parties in the election of 1840 were named by conventions. Conventions were special meetings called for that particular purpose. Before 1840 candidates generally had been chosen by members of their party in Congress.

The Democrats nominated President Van Buren for a second term. The Whigs chose a military hero, William Henry Harrison. Harrison had commanded the troops that defeated Tecumseh's Indians at Tippecanoe in 1811. For Vice-President, the Whigs chose John Tyler of Virginia. He was not a Whig, but a Southerner who opposed Jackson and was in favor of states' rights. The Whigs favored a national bank, a high tariff and many roads, canals, and railways.

The Whigs were well organized and they won the election. They tried to get the vote of the average man. Harrison had once lived in a log cabin and he drank hard cider. This made him a "man of the people." His victory over the Indians at Tippecanoe had made him a hero. The Whigs made so much of these things that the campaign of 1840 became known as the "log cabin, hard cider campaign." The Whig slogan was "Tippecanoe and Tyler too." The country was still in a depression, and President Van Buren and the Democrats were blamed for the hard times. The Whig victory was the result of this condition plus a rousing campaign.

Unhappily for the Whigs, President Harrison died a few months after he was inaugurated. Tyler became President. When the Whigs in Congress voted for a national bank, Tyler vetoed the bill. Tyler also did not approve of internal improvements. All the Whigs in Tyler's Cabinet resigned in disgust. Secretary of State Daniel Webster stayed on for a few months to wind up an agreement with England that settled the boundary between Maine and Canada. Then Webster resigned too.

The major question for the United States was now a new one. How far west should the nation expand?

REVIEW ACTIVITIES

1. What events made the federal government stronger after 1815?
2. The "electorate" are the people who vote. How did the electorate in 1828 differ from the electorate in 1790?
3. Why was South Carolina for "nullification?"

4. What were some of the causes of the Panic of 1837?
5. How did Jackson's policies differ from those of President John Quincy Adams?

Select the words that best complete the following sentences. (*Please do not write in this book.*)

1. Factory owners asked the federal government for _____. They wanted a high _____.
2. In the case of McCulloch versus Maryland, Chief Justice _____ said that Congress had "implied power" to set up a _____ _____.
3. President _____ declaration that no foreign state ought to try to put any more colonies in America is called the _____ _____.
4. In the election of 1824 _____ _____ _____ was elected President. Because electoral votes were tied, he was elected by the House of _____.
5. The _____ Canal in _____ _____ State provides cheap transportation for goods going to and from the West.

Who or what were the following:

1. Democratic—Republicans
2. Eli Whitney
3. Henry Clay
4. Robert Fulton
5. Spoils System

CHAPTER 8

Winning the West

SETTLERS SPREAD THEIR IDEAS OF FREEDOM AND DEMOCRACY THROUGH THE WEST

The men and women who came to live in America had a special dream, a special hope. The Pilgrims and the Puritans dreamed of a new "City of God." Sin was to have no place in their America. During the War for Independence, men dreamed of a new republic, a safe place for liberty. America would be a home for all people who wanted freedom.

The new nation became independent. It prospered and it grew larger. The idea spread that America had a special role to play in the world. Americans were proud of their freedom, their prosperity and their democratic government. They thought that a country such as theirs should spread over the whole continent and become a great force in the world.

Of course not every American felt this way, but there

were many who did. When their countrymen traveled west to trade and to clear the lands, they believed it was right that the United States government go with them. It seemed proper to spread our special ideas of freedom and democracy across America to the Pacific Ocean. This was the way America had grown from the beginning.

The new nation won western lands from England. It bought Louisiana from France and Florida from Spain. In little more than fifty years, the number of states had doubled and the population had increased ten times over.

Texans Fought for Independence from Mexico

The Panic of 1837 did not stop Americans from moving west. Instead, it even encouraged some to move beyond the borders of the Louisiana Purchase. Americans began to migrate to the Oregon Territory, which was occupied by the United States and England together. They started to settle in California, which was then part of Mexico. For years Americans had been streaming into what is now the state of Texas.

Texas was once part of the Spanish colony of Mexico. Then Mexico revolted and became independent. In 1822 Mexico allowed an American, Stephen Austin, to found a colony in Texas. Land was cheap and cotton would grow on it. By 1830, over 20,000 Americans with slaves had followed Austin into the Mexican province of Texas. Mexico began to fear that the Americans in Texas were becoming too powerful.

The government of Mexico wanted to stop this. So it said that no new settlements could be founded in Texas. The Mexican government also made it illegal to bring slaves into Texas and placed a tariff on American goods. The Americans in Texas rebelled. In March of 1836, the Mexican General Santa Anna wiped out a Texan force at the Alamo Mission in San Antonio. Both Davy Crockett, the famous scout, and James Bowie, inventor of the Bowie knife, were killed in this battle. Later that year, Texans defeated the Mexican army and declared themselves independent.

For ten years Texas remained an independent republic. More Americans settled in the new country, and it seemed natural that Texas would join the Union. But President Jackson did not invite Texas to become a state. He feared that such a step might result in a war with Mexico. Then, too, there were slaves in Texas, and many Northerners did not want another slave state.

SLAVERY IN THE NEW TERRITORIES WAS A PROBLEM

As the United States grew larger and stronger after the War of 1812, differences appeared in three sections of the country. In the Northeast, manufacturing and shipping were important. The West grew mostly meat and grain. The South grew cotton. To pick the cotton, the Southerners used Negro slaves.

Before the War of Independence, human slaves were bought and sold in all American colonies. After the war, slavery was ended in the North. In the South, slaves were kept to farm tobacco and pick cotton. Many Northerners thought that slavery was wrong and wanted to see it stopped. However, southern farmers and planters felt that they could not do without slaves.

In 1818 Missouri asked to be admitted to the Union. A northern congressman declared that Missouri should be admitted only if its slaves were freed. At this time the number of "slave states" equaled the number of states where there were no slaves. If Missouri became a "free state," Congress would have two more senators to vote against slavery. The southern states objected. They argued that there had always been slaves in the Louisiana Territory, and that Congress had no right to end slavery there.

In 1820 Congress agreed to a compromise known as the Missouri Compromise. Missouri would become a state where slavery was permitted. At the same time, Massachusetts would be divided into two separate states. The northern part would enter the Union as the free state of Maine. Thus the number of senators from slave states and free states would remain equal. It was agreed that farther west the line between new slave states and new free states would be drawn along the southern boundary of Missouri.

From 1820 on, states were admitted in pairs. Arkansas became a state in 1836 and Michigan in 1837. If Texas were admitted, the balance would be upset in favor of the slave states.

SETTLEMENT OF LAND CLAIMED BY ENGLAND AND MEXICO RAISED NEW QUESTIONS

Meanwhile, Americans were moving into Oregon. After the War of 1812, England and the United States had failed to agree on any boundary west of the Rocky Mountains. The Oregon Territory extended from the Rocky Mountains to the Pacific Ocean and from the northern end of California to the southern tip of Alaska. This territory was "jointly occupied" by the United States and England.

For many years the only white men in the Northwest were English fur traders. Then American fur traders followed the route of Lewis and Clark into Oregon. Christian missionaries went to the Northwest to convert the Indians. During the bad years after the Panic of 1837, farmers and settlers crossed the Oregon Trail to live in the Columbia and Willamette River valleys. Could the United States now claim this land? Would England give it up?

Farther south, pioneers settled in Mexican territory near the Great Salt Lake. These people were members of a religious sect called Mormons. Americans who did not like

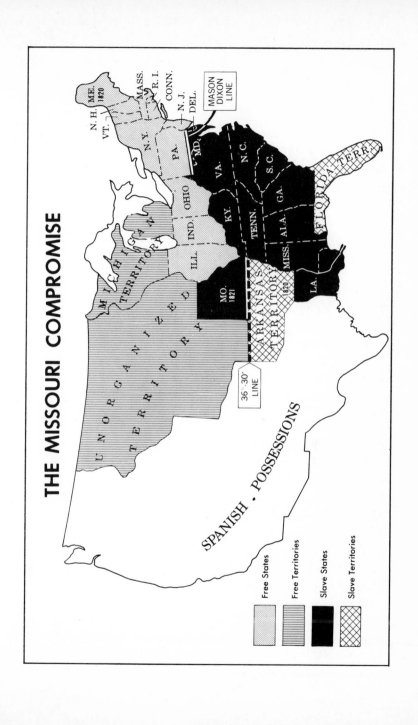

THE MISSOURI COMPROMISE

MASON
DIXON
LINE

36°-30' LINE

N. H.
VT.
ME.
1820
MASS.
R. I.
CONN.
N. Y.
N. J.
DEL.
PA.
MD.
VA.
N. C.
S. C.
GA.
FLORIDA TERR.
KY.
TENN.
ALA.
MISS.
LA.
OHIO
IND.
ILL.
MICHIGAN TERRITORY
MO.
1821
ARKANSAS TERRITORY
1820
U N O R G A N I Z E D   T E R R I T O R Y

SPANISH · POSSESSIONS

Free States

Free Territories

Slave States

Slave Territories

the Mormons drove them out of Ohio and Illinois. The Mormons followed the Oregon Trail as far as the Rocky Mountains. In 1847 they set up a colony near the Great Salt Lake in what is now the state of Utah. The Mormons built roads and irrigation canals, and turned what had been desert into a profitable colony.

Even before this, American traders in covered wagons crossed trails west of Missouri to buy and sell in the Mexican town of Santa Fe. Still farther west, Americans were living in the coastal towns of California, which was then part of Mexico. Against Mexican law, they settled on farms in the Sacramento River valley.

MANIFEST DESTINY BECAME AN ISSUE IN THE ELECTION OF 1844

Were all these people destined to belong to another country? Should not the United States govern and protect them? Should not the United States claim all the land westward to the Pacific? It looked right on the map. The settlers were Americans. The land was rich in many places. That America should grow in this direction seemed decided by fate. When writing about it, one newspaper said that it was America's *manifest destiny* to take over all the land as far as the Pacific. Mexico and the claims of England were all that stood in the way of western expansion.

These questions were being asked during the last months of Tyler's presidency. The Whigs, who had won the election of 1840, were against adding more land to the Union. They objected especially to the addition of Texas because Texas allowed slavery. Then, too, the admission of Texas might lead to war with Mexico.

Other Americans, particularly those in the South, favored this expansion. The United States and Texas were part of the same land area. Only a small river separated Texas from Louisiana. It was as natural, they thought, to add Texas to the Union as it had been to buy Louisiana or Florida.

The Democrats, followers of Jackson, were enthusiastic about expansion. Not only did they want Texas in the Union, but they wanted to add all of Oregon as well. Americans in Texas said they wanted to join the Union. And in 1843 American settlers in Oregon set up their own government and waited for the United States to claim the territory.

The Democrats agreed with the settlers. They nominated James K. Polk for President in 1844 and demanded the "re-annexation" of Texas, and the "re-occupation" of Oregon. Polk and the Democrats won the election.

John Tyler, who was President after Harrison died, was a Southerner, and he wanted Texas in the Union. He made a treaty annexing Texas, but Whigs in the Senate had turned it down. Then after Polk was elected, but before he could take office, Congress quickly made Texas a state by a joint resolution of both Houses.

The United States and England Compromised on the Oregon Territory

President Polk informed Great Britain that joint occupation of the Oregon Territory should end. The northern boundary of the territory was near Alaska. On the map it is measured at 54 degrees and 40 minutes north latitude. Polk suggested to England that the territory be divided between Canada and the United States. When England refused to give up the southern half, Americans demanded the entire territory. "Fifty-four forty, or fight," the Americans shouted.

Both countries pretended to prepare for war. Then they signed a treaty in 1846 to divide the Oregon Territory at the 49th parallel. That was what Polk had suggested in the first place. Through this treaty, the United States obtained the land that is now the states of Oregon and Washington.

Elsewhere, things did not go so peacefully. Soon America was at war with Mexico, just as the Whigs had feared.

Nobody knew the exact boundary between Texas and the rest of Mexico. Texans claimed it was the Rio Grande. Mexicans said it was the Nueces River. President Polk sent a special minister, John Slidell, to Mexico City to settle this matter.

Slidell offered money to the Mexican government in exchange for its agreement that the Rio Grande was the proper boundary. Slidell also was prepared to buy California. But he was unsuccessful. Then President Polk ordered an army led by General Zachary Taylor to go to the Rio Grande. The Mexican government claimed that General Taylor was on Mexican soil. When he refused to leave, a Mexican army attacked. After this incident, Congress declared war on Mexico. Only a few Whigs and men who were against slavery objected to the war.

The United States won the war against Mexico in less than two years. General Taylor's soldiers marched across the Rio Grande. They defeated Mexican armies at Monterey and then at Buena Vista. This ended the fighting in northern Mexico.

Meanwhile, part of Taylor's army had sailed to central Mexico with General Winfield Scott. Scott's army captured Vera Cruz and fought all the way into Mexico City. Farther north, a small army led by General Philip Kearny took Santa Fe in New Mexico and marched overland to capture San Diego in California. Americans living in California rebelled against Mexico and set up the free state of California. Mexico lost on all fronts. Some people talked about taking all of Mexico. Newspaper articles, many army and navy officers, and several congressmen all urged Polk to annex the whole country. More moderate views won out, however, and in

February of 1848, a treaty was signed at Guadalupe-Hidalgo.

The United States Gained New Territories in the Southwest

The treaty that ended the Mexican War put the boundary of Texas at the Rio Grande. Mexico gave up all of California and all of the land between California and Texas. That gave the United States the area that is now Arizona, New Mexico, Utah, Nevada and part of Colorado and Wyoming. In return, the United States paid Mexico 15 million dollars and agreed to repay all Americans to whom Mexico owed money.

After 1848 the United States occupied a solid strip of land that stretched across the continent. The nation had signed a treaty with England over the Oregon Territory. She had won the war against Mexico. The government was strong, and the country was free to grow. The country did grow, both in numbers and in wealth. But the question of slavery still divided it.

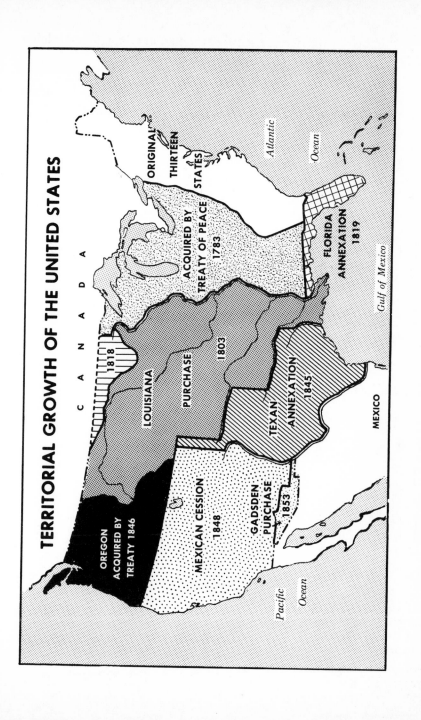

TERRITORIAL GROWTH OF THE UNITED STATES

C A N A D A

ORIGINAL
THIRTEEN
STATES

ACQUIRED BY
TREATY OF PEACE
1783

1818

LOUISIANA
PURCHASE
1803

OREGON
ACQUIRED BY
TREATY 1846

MEXICAN CESSION
1848

GADSDEN
PURCHASE
1853

TEXAN
ANNEXATION
1845

FLORIDA
ANNEXATION
1819

MEXICO

Atlantic

Ocean

Gulf of Mexico

Pacific

Ocean

REVIEW ACTIVITIES

1. Why did Mexico object to Americans settling in Texas? What did Mexico do to stop them?
2. What was the Missouri Compromise of 1820? What did it accomplish?
3. What was meant by *manifest destiny?*
4. When people shouted "Fifty-four forty, or fight," what did they mean?
5. What territories did the United States win from Mexico?

Select the words that best complete the following sentences. (*Please do not write in this book.*)

1. The Mexican general who defeated the Texans at the _____ _____ was _____ _____.
2. The Oregon Territory extended from the _____ Mountains to the Pacific Ocean, and from the northern end of _____ to the southern tip of Alaska.
3. In 1844 the _____ followed the _____ Trail to the Rockies and set up their religious colony in Utah.
4. Whigs did not want to annex _____ because it would be a _____ state.
5. In 1844 the _____ Party nominated James K. _____ for president.

Who or what were the following:

1. Stephen Austin
2. 49th Parallel
3. John Slidell
4. Rio Grande
5. Zachary Taylor

CHAPTER 9

How the War Between the States Began

SLAVERY IN NEW TERRITORIES REMAINED A PROBLEM

While America was winning new territories, the argument over slavery was dividing the nation. Finally it led to a civil war.

The Missouri Compromise of 1820 had settled the issue of slavery in the Louisiana Territory, but it did not cover slavery in the new territories. Besides, it was only a political settlement that did not say whether slavery was right or wrong. But more people began to believe that slavery was wrong.

Anti-slavery societies that had started during the War for Independence now grew rapidly. Their main goal was to prevent slavery from spreading. Some men wanted to completely wipe out or abolish slavery. They were known as *abolitionists*. Among most people the abolitionists were unpopular. Their program was too radical and too sudden. One abolitionist, a Boston editor named William Lloyd

Garrison, was dragged through the streets by a mob. Another, a publisher and preacher named Elijah Lovejoy, was killed by a mob in Illinois. That shows how strongly people felt about the issue of slavery.

Soon after the Mexican War began, many people began to wonder if slavery would be allowed in the new territories. Or would it be forbidden? Abolitionists believed that slavery should be forbidden.

There Were Several Proposals for Settling the Slavery Question

When Congress was about to vote money to finish up the Mexican War, Representative David Wilmot of Pennsylvania proposed that the money be voted only if slavery were made illegal in any new territories won from Mexico. The *Wilmot Proviso*, as this proposal was called, was popular in the North and West. It would mean that no more slave states would enter the Union. Of course the South was against the proposal. In Congress, Wilmot's Proviso was brought up several times, but it never became a law.

There were two other ways to deal with slavery in the new territories. One was to divide the land into two sections—one slave and one free. The Missouri Compromise had divided the Louisiana Territory in this way at the 36th parallel. President Polk suggested that the line be extended to the Pacific Ocean. That was one solution.

The other method was to let the people who lived in the new territories decide the issue for themselves. This method is known as *popular sovereignty*. Slave owners in the South did not like the idea. They feared that popular sovereignty would result in votes against slavery.

In the presidential election of 1848, the Democratic Party was badly divided over the issue of slavery in the new territories. The Whig Party straddled the issue. Their presidential candidate was a war hero, General Zachary

Taylor. He was a Southerner and a slave owner. The Whig candidate for Vice-President was Millard Fillmore of New York. Fillmore opposed slavery in the new territories. Thus the Whigs had candidates on both sides of the fence. They won the election.

Congress Passed the Compromise of 1850

The Whigs faced the question of slavery in the territories as soon as they took office. California asked to enter the Union as a free state.

Gold had been discovered in the Sacramento River valley in California—lots and lots of gold. It was lying in the beds of streams, and it was easy to mine. The news spread quickly. During 1849 men from all over the world flocked to California to mine gold. They were called *Forty-Niners*.

Soon there were 100,000 new settlers in California. They were miners and traders, not planters and slave owners. The settlers drew up a form of government without slavery and asked that California be made a state. In Congress, California's request brought to a head the argument between slave states and free states.

Slavery in the territories was not the only question. There were other parts to the argument over slavery. And Southerners saw little chance of getting their way in any of them. Many slaves were escaping to the North. Officials in the northern states did not always enforce the law and return runaway slaves to their owners. If they tried to, abolitionists hid the slaves and sent them on to Canada at night. Abolitionists thought that they were doing right. Slave owners thought that the abolitionists were stealing, and they wanted their property back.

Another sore spot was Washington, D.C. Human slaves were bought and sold in the nation's capital. Northerners did not like this practice; they felt it was a national shame. In the Southwest, the slave state of Texas claimed half of the

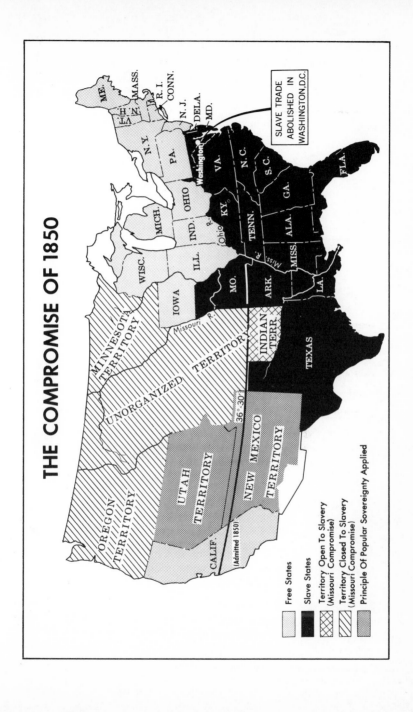

THE COMPROMISE OF 1850

SLAVE TRADE ABOLISHED IN WASHINGTON, D.C.

Free States

Slave States

Territory Open To Slavery (Missouri Compromise)

Territory Closed To Slavery (Missouri Compromise)

Principle Of Popular Sovereignty Applied

territory of New Mexico. But the federal government refused to recognize Texas's claim.

Southerners were on the verge of losing all of these arguments. They began to talk seriously about leaving the Union. Then Henry Clay suggested a compromise, known as the *Compromise of 1850*. Because Clay's proposal contained so many parts, it was called an "omnibus" bill.

The main points were these: 1) California would enter the Union as a free state; 2) in the other territories won from Mexico, the people living there would decide if it would be free or slave—they would follow popular sovereignty; 3) Texas would not claim New Mexico and, in return, the federal government would pay the money that Texas owed as a result of her war with Mexico; 4) no more slaves would be bought or sold in the nation's capital; 5) a strict law to cover runaway slaves would be enforced by federal officials.

Each of Clay's proposals pleased one side and displeased the other. In Congress, the debate lasted all summer. Senator Daniel Webster, although he was a Whig and a Northerner, spoke in favor of the Compromise in order to save the Union.

In the middle of the debate, President Taylor died and Millard Fillmore became President. Fillmore worked hard for the Compromise. Although many northern Whigs were against it to the end, Clay's Compromise was finally adopted. For the moment, the South was content.

The Compromise of 1850 was a practical solution. It did not entirely satisfy anyone. Northerners especially did not like the law about runaway, or fugitive, slaves. Sometimes they even prevented federal officers from enforcing the law. But for the sake of peace, most people accepted the Compromise.

The Democratic Party was united in supporting the Compromise, and they won the election of 1852. The new President was Franklin Pierce. Inside of two years, however, the whole question of slavery in the territories arose again. This time the problem was how to organize the territories of Kansas and Nebraska.

The Kansas-Nebraska Act Led to a Tragic Situation

Nebraska was Indian territory. But farmers wanted to settle there, and Chicago businessmen wanted to build a railroad through Nebraska to California. They wanted farmers in Nebraska, not Indians. In Congress, Senator Stephen Douglas of Illinois proposed that the Indians be driven out of Kansas and Nebraska. He proposed that this land be made into federal territories open to farmers.

Douglas needed southern votes for his proposal, but he knew that southern senators would not vote for new territories that forbade slavery. Under the Missouri Compromise slavery was forbidden in the northern part of the Louisiana Territory. So Douglas proposed that the Missouri Compromise be repealed. He also proposed that the question of slavery in the new territories be decided by popular sovereignty.

Southerners supported Douglas's proposals, and the Kansas-Nebraska Act was passed. Northerners who opposed the spread of slavery were furious. Many northern Democrats joined with former Whigs to organize a new party that would oppose the spread of slavery. They called themselves Republicans. The new Republican Party won so many votes in the election of 1854 that they controlled the House of Representatives.

What happened in Kansas was tragic. Of the two new territories, only Kansas was far enough south to attract slave owners. Pioneers from slave states and free states rushed to settle there. On election day, pro-slavery men from Missouri crossed the Kansas border and helped to elect a pro-slavery legislature.

As months passed, anti-slavery men greatly outnumbered

pro-slavery men in Kansas. They set up a legislature of their own. Both legislatures drew up state constitutions—one slave, the other free. Soon a small civil war began. Pro-slavery men attacked the town of Lawrence and burned it. In return, anti-slavery fanatics led by John Brown murdered six pro-slavery settlers. Within the next three years, some 200 people lost their lives.

THE REPUBLICAN PARTY MADE A GOOD SHOWING IN THE ELECTION OF 1856

Many northern Democrats were unhappy with the Kansas-Nebraska Act. But in the election of 1856 they agreed to accept it in order to keep the country united. The Democrats nominated James Buchanan of Pennsylvania for President. Buchanan had not been involved with the passing of the Kansas-Nebraska Act.

The new Republican Party made the trouble in Kansas the big issue of the campaign. They opposed the Kansas-Nebraska Act. They were for keeping slavery out of all federal territories. They appealed to northern Democrats who were against slavery. They also appealed to what was left of the old Whig Party of Henry Clay and Daniel Webster. The Republican presidential candidate was John C. Fremont, a general and an explorer.

The Republican Party made a good showing, but the Democrats won. Buchanan became the new President.

President Buchanan needed to keep the southern Democrats content with the Union. He said that Kansas should vote on the pro-slavery constitution first. But by the time a vote was taken in 1857, anti-slavery men outnumbered the others. They voted against the pro-slavery constitution. Southern senators, however, would not vote to admit Kansas as a free state. So Kansas had to wait before it could be admitted to the Union.

The Missouri Compromise Was Overruled

That same year, 1857, in the Dred Scott decision, the Supreme Court had ruled that nobody had the right to forbid slavery in any United States territory. Dred Scott was a slave who had lived with his master for a time in the northern part of the Louisiana Territory where slavery was forbidden. After he went home to the South, his master died, and he asked the courts for his freedom. The case came to the Supreme Court. Chief Justice Roger Taney and the Supreme Court decided that Scott was still a slave. Chief Justice Taney went on to explain that Congress had no right to outlaw slavery in the territories. In other words, Taney said that the Missouri Compromise was unconstitutional, and there was no way to end slavery except by state law.

Slave owners were pleased with the Dred Scott decision. Abolitionists were angry. The Republican Party was worried. Its political platform was based on opposition to slavery in the territories. The Republicans wanted to have Chief Justice Taney's decision changed.

LINCOLN AND DOUGLAS DEBATED THE SLAVERY QUESTION

The election of 1858 came during the excitement over Kansas and the Dred Scott decision. Senator Douglas of Illinois was up for re-election. He was responsible for the Kansas-Nebraska Act. He said that popular sovereignty was the way to handle slavery. To oppose him, the Republicans nominated Abraham Lincoln, an Illinois lawyer.

Lincoln was born in a log cabin in Kentucky. For a time he lived in Indiana and then in Illinois. His parents were poor and young Lincoln did not go to school much. But he read all the books he could get his hands on, and thus he became a self-educated man. He was tall and homely; yet he became one of the most successful lawyers in the state of Illinois. Before the election of 1858, Lincoln challenged

Douglas to a series of debates which have become famous.

Both Lincoln and Douglas wanted to be elected as senator from Illinois. Douglas not only wanted to be re-elected senator, but he also wanted to lead the entire Democratic Party and become their presidential candidate in 1860. During a debate in the town of Freeport, Illinois, Lincoln brought up the question of slavery in the territories. What stand would Douglas take? You remember that the Kansas-Nebraska Act said that people in the territories could decide for themselves whether or not slavery would be permitted. The Supreme Court, on the other hand, declared that nobody could forbid slavery in a United States territory. Which, Lincoln asked Douglas, was right?

If Douglas said the Supreme Court was right, the southern Democrats would like him, but he might lose the election in Illinois. If he said people could exclude slavery from a territory, he would please the Illinois voters, but southern Democrats would not approve. What Douglas said at Freeport amounted to the following: legally, you could not outlaw slavery in a territory, but, practically, you could refuse to protect slave owners, and that would amount to the same thing. Douglas won the election and retained his seat in the Senate. But the South was not satisfied with his answer at Freeport. They wanted slavery made legal and protected in the territories.

Two years later when the Democrats met to nominate their presidential candidate, southern Democrats refused to support Senator Douglas.

THE ABOLITION MOVEMENT GREW IN THE NORTH

Meanwhile, the situation in Kansas grew quiet. Most of the settlers there opposed slavery. It became clear that when Kansas finally entered the Union it would be as a free state. The question of whether or not slavery would be legal and protected in the territories seemed almost settled.

But abolitionists wanted to see slavery ended altogether. In 1852 Harriet Beecher Stowe had published a novel, *Uncle Tom's Cabin,* that dramatically showed the worst side of slavery. *Uncle Tom's Cabin* was a best-seller. It persuaded many people to become abolitionists.

Then in 1859 John Brown, one of the anti-slavery leaders in Kansas, tried to start a slave uprising in the South. He planned to set up a refuge for runaway slaves. Brown wanted to form an army that he could use to free the remaining slaves. He and his followers captured the United States arsenal at Harper's Ferry in Virginia. They wanted guns for the slaves to use in their revolution. John Brown was captured a day later by the Virginia militia, and he was tried and hanged for treason. Southerners felt that John Brown's actions and hopes represented all northern abolitionists.

Then came the election of 1860. By this time, the Republican Party had grown larger. But it was strong only in the northern and western parts of the country. The Republican Party stood for everything that separated the North from the South.

THE NORTH AND SOUTH HAD MANY DIFFERENCES

Slavery was not the only difference between the North and South. They differed in population and in industry, and their interests were not the same.

After the Mexican War, industry grew much faster in the North than it did in the South. The first railroads were opened for public business in 1830 when Andrew Jackson was President. By the early 1850's, four different railroad lines reached from eastern seaports into Ohio. There were 10,000 miles of track, most of which was in the North. Within the next ten years, the amount of railroad track had doubled. The sewing machine, invented in the 1840's, speeded up the manufacture of clothing and shoes. The manufacture of reapers and other farm machinery became a big business during the 1850's. More than 15,000 new factories were started during those ten years. Factory owners wanted a protective tariff.

Most of the new factories were in the North. The South remained agricultural. In the South, 8,000 miles of railroad track were laid in the late 1850's. Traffic on the Mississippi River was heavy and profitable. But southern money was tied up in slaves and in land for growing cotton. There was not enough money left over to put into factories. Southern industry lagged far behind northern industry. This divided the North and the South on many other issues.

Recall the issues that had been important before—the protective tariff, the National Bank, internal improvements, and the sale of western lands. On each of these issues there was strong feeling in the North that ran against the views of the South. There was no industry in the South to demand protection. Cotton planters wanted to buy their manufactured goods as cheaply as possible. They did not want to pay a tariff just to protect northern factories. The South wanted a low tariff.

Although the small farmer in the North and West liked the easy credit that state banks gave him, the new industrial class in the North wanted stricter banking practices. They favored the idea of national controls. Southern farmers wanted easy credit from local banks. For some time the use of national money to build roads and railroads and to improve rivers and harbors had been considered proper. Most of these improvements, however, helped the North and West more than the South. Southerners began to regard such improvements as a way to weaken the South's share in the nation's business.

Finally, the way to sell western land to settlers became an issue. Westerners wanted this land to be sold cheaply or given away in small farms. At first eastern factory owners were against the giving away of land. They were afraid they would lose the workers to whom they paid low wages. But by the 1850's they had changed their minds. It turned out that, because of immigrants, there were plenty of workers.

More and more immigrants were coming to America. They numbered about 100,000 per year in the 1840's. Ten years later they were arriving at the rate of 350,000 a year. Few immigrants went south to compete with slave labor. Many of them stayed in the North to work in factories. Others traveled west in search of farms. Southerners could see that a policy of free land would make the North and West grow rapidly. Free land in the West might mean that more non-slave states would enter the Union. Therefore, the South opposed the free-land policy.

The Election of 1860 Helped to Divide the Nation Even Further

On every issue, the Republican Party took a stand that was popular in the North but unpopular in the South. Republicans opposed slavery in the territories. They were against admitting additional slave states. Republicans were for protective tariffs. They were for internal improvements. They favored free land for western settlers. They promised to observe the fugitive slave law, but they wanted that law to be less rigid. Resenting all of this, many Southerners thought the South should leave the Union if a Republican were elected President.

In 1860 the Republicans nominated Abraham Lincoln for President. The Democrats could not agree either on a candidate or on the issue of slavery. Their convention split in two. Northern Democrats nominated Senator Douglas, who favored popular sovereignty. Southern Democrats named John Breckinridge of Kentucky, who wanted slavery protected in the territories. Breckinridge said that if Lincoln were elected

President, the South should leave the Union. John Bell of Tennessee represented Southerners who wanted to preserve the Union and would have nothing to do with secession. He became the fourth presidential candidate.

Because the Democratic vote was so divided, Lincoln won every electoral vote in the North and West. Only forty per cent of the people voted for him, but he received sixty per cent of the electoral votes.

Southern States Established the Confederacy

To the South, Lincoln's election seemed a disaster. Southerners had absolutely no voice in the Republican Party. A party that represented only the North would be running the nation. This had never happened before. There had always been southern leaders in both the Whig and the Democratic Parties. Thus far, nine out of the fifteen Presidents had come from the South. Now the South would have to submit to all the laws that were passed by Northerners. They decided they would not do this.

Before Lincoln took office, South Carolina and six other southern states withdrew from the Union. They drew up a constitution much like that of the United States. But they made slavery legal and protective tariffs illegal. They called themselves the Confederate States of America and elected Jefferson Davis of Mississippi as their President. Southerners began to seize all national property in their states. They took over 200,000 guns stored in federal arsenals in the South. This was the situation when Lincoln became the President in March, 1861.

REVIEW ACTIVITIES

1. What national problems were settled by the Compromise of 1850? How did the Compromise meet the issues?

2. How did the Kansas-Nebraska Act change the Missouri Compromise?
3. In the Lincoln-Douglas debates, what was the main argument about?
4. How did the economy—that is, business conditions—differ between North and South in the 1850's?
5. Why did Southerners object to giving free land to western settlers?

Select the words that best complete the following sentences. (*Please do not write in this book.*)

1. Men who wished to wipe out ——————— were called ———————.
2. Men who rushed to California to mine ——————— were called ———————.
3. Senator Daniel Webster ——————— the Compromise of 1850 "in order to save the ———————."
4. The Republican Party had grown strong in the ——————— and ——————— parts of the country at the time of the election of 1860.
5. ——————— ——————— and six other southern states formed the ——————— States of America.

Who or what were the following:

1. Wilmot Proviso
2. Popular Sovereignty
3. James Buchanan
4. Dred Scott
5. John Brown

CHAPTER **10**

The War Between the States

LINCOLN BECAME PRESIDENT OF A DIVIDED COUNTRY

When Abraham Lincoln took office in March of 1861, the country was divided. Seven states already had left the Union and four more withdrew the following month. In his inaugural address, Lincoln said that he had no right to end slavery. He urged the southern states to return to the Union. Instead, Confederate forces fired on United States soldiers at Fort Sumter in the harbor of Charleston, South Carolina. The commander of Fort Sumter held out for two days. Then on April 13 he surrendered. Two days later President Lincoln called for 75,000 volunteer soldiers. He ordered the Union Navy to prevent all ships from entering or leaving seaports in southern states. War had begun.

Until this time, many Northerners had no idea what should be done about the southern states. Some felt sorry for the South. Anti-slavery people were glad to be rid of the slave states. They thought that the "erring sisters" should be allowed to depart in peace. The cannon shots at Fort Sumter changed all that. Most Northerners now felt that the Union had been attacked. Volunteers signed up for the Union Army.

What would the other slave states do? Virginia, North Carolina, Tennessee and Arkansas joined the Confederacy. Four slave states, Kentucky, Maryland, Delaware, and Missouri, were cautious and remained in the Union. Officially, the war was not about slavery. Officially, the question was whether or not a few states had the right to withdraw from the Union.

A Long War Set In

During the spring of 1861, both sides raised armies, and thousands of untrained volunteers filled the ranks. Everyone believed that the fighting would end within a few months. Northerners were impatient to win the war. They wanted the Union Army to conquer Richmond, the capital of the Confederacy. But the army that finally tried an attack in July of 1861 was beaten by the Confederates at Bull Run. In disorder, Union soldiers and crowds of people who went out to watch fled toward Washington.

After this, President Lincoln and the northern leaders realized that they were in for a long fight. They planned for war in three main areas. First, the Union would try to defeat the Confederate Army in Virginia and capture Richmond. Second, in the West, the Union would try to control the main rivers, especially the Mississippi River. If they were successful, Texas and Arkansas would be cut off from the rest of the South. Finally, the Union Navy would try to prevent all ships from entering or leaving southern ports. This "blockade" would keep the South from importing food and supplies. The plan was a good one, but it took four years to work it out.

The North Had Superior Resources

At first it seemed that victory would be an easy matter. The North had many advantages. The twenty-three states of the Union had a population of more than 22 million. The eleven states of the Confederacy had only 9 million people, one-third of whom were Negro slaves. In addition, the majority of factories, banks and ships were in the North. Northern farms produced enough meat and grain to feed the entire nation. Most of the American railroads were in the North. They linked factories in the East with farms in the West. The Union also had most of the United States Navy.

By contrast, the South had always imported meat and grain from the West. And they bought their manufactured goods from the North and from Europe. The main activity in the South was the growing of cotton and tobacco. These products would be of little help in winning a war. Why then did the war last so long?

One reason was that the northern armies had to invade the South, capture forts and cities and occupy land. This was much harder to do than for the South to defend land already held. The South had fine generals who made few mistakes. The Union Navy was not large enough to close all southern ports completely. Many ships "ran the blockade" and brought needed supplies to the South.

The *Merrimac* Threatened the North's Blockade

At one time the South almost broke up the entire blockade. Confederates took an old wooden ship, the *Merrimac*, and covered it with iron sheets. Then they put a big iron point, or "ram," in the prow. In March of 1862 this strange ship steamed into the Union naval base at Hampton Roads. The Union ships fired their guns, but the old-fashioned cannon balls bounced off the *Merrimac*'s sides. The *Merrimac* sank one Union warship and captured another. The Union, however, had built its own "ironclad." This was a small ship called the *Monitor*. It had only two guns inside a closed plat-form that could be turned around. These two strange ships fought a battle. Neither ship could sink the other. But the *Merrimac* did not come out to fight again.

A few Confederate warships escaped into the open seas. They hunted northern merchant ships which they cap-tured or sank. Three warships were built for the South in Great Britain, even though it was illegal for the British gov-ernment to allow this. After the war, Britain paid for all damage to American shipping that was caused by these three ships. But at the time, British merchants and owners of cot-ton mills wanted the South to win the war. Only when it became clear that the South would lose, did England stop building warships for the South. However, this was not until 1863. Meanwhile northern armies had been unable to defeat the South.

Lee Kept the Union Armies at Bay

Union troops under General George B. McClellan ad-vanced almost to Richmond during the first year of the war. But the Confederate Army drove them back. The next year, 1862, the North had a new general, John Pope. Pope and his soldiers were badly beaten at a second battle near Bull Run. The Confederate Army of Virginia, under the command of General Robert E. Lee, marched northward toward Pennsylvania. The two armies met near Antietam in Maryland in a bloody battle that neither side won. General Lee retreated to Virginia. After nearly two years of war, the situation in Virginia had undergone little change. The North could not beat General Lee's armies, nor could they occupy much Confederate territory.

Northern Forces Were Successful in the West

Conditions were different in the West. Early in 1862 a small western army commanded by General Ulysses S.

Grant marched south from Illinois. It captured forts on the Tennessee and Cumberland Rivers and occupied most of western Tennessee. Grant's army was almost beaten in a fierce battle at Shiloh, but the southern general was killed and his army retreated into Mississippi. Grant's army then took over Memphis on the Mississippi River.

At the same time, Union ships and soldiers captured New Orleans. Only a small section of the Mississippi River remained in Confederate hands.

The North Had to Use Special War Measures

The war was far from over. Resistance in the South was still firm. The North needed to bring more of its great strength into play.

President Lincoln realized that the North needed a better "cause." It was hard for people to fight just to "preserve the Union." Many people thought that the war was really against slavery. If that cause could be admitted openly, the Northerners would have an ideal to fight for. Also, liberals in England would then support the North rather than the South. President Lincoln had said he could not free the slaves in all the states. As a war measure, however, he could free the slaves in enemy territory. After the battle at Antietam, he did just that. Lincoln issued his *Emancipation Proclamation*. This statement declared that after January 1, 1863, all slaves were to be freed in those states where the people were in rebellion.

The Emancipation Proclamation did not put an end to slavery. Slavery was still allowed in the states that had remained in the Union. It was even allowed in areas such as Louisiana and western Tennessee that had already been conquered. But the proclamation pleased the North. And it made the British government more friendly toward the Union cause.

More than just a cause was needed, however. The war

required supplies, men and money. Supplies were furnished by the farms which had good crops, and by factories which grew rapidly in order to meet the war-time demand. But the war required more soldiers than the northern leaders had thought. For two years there were enough volunteers, but by 1863 more men were needed. Congress passed a draft law in March of 1863. All able-bodied men between 18 and 45 could be called for service. If a rich man was drafted, however, he usually could buy his way out. Poor people in New York and Boston did not like the draft and they staged riots against it. But it was enforced until the end of the war.

War expenses for the North were more than 2 million dollars a day. The government raised the tariff rates and put a tax on almost everything. The government also printed paper money, called *greenbacks*. But most of the war costs were met by borrowing money.

Congress set up a system of national banks partly to sell bonds and partly to get a sound currency. The National Banking Act of 1863 did not set up one national bank. It set up rules for local banks to obtain a national charter. One rule said that the local bank had to buy government bonds. The bank then used these bonds to back up its own bank notes. This system of banking lasted until 1913.

Not everybody in the North favored the war. There were many Northerners who thought the South should win. These men were called *copperheads*. President Lincoln had to use his war powers to keep the copperheads in check. He took away their constitutional right to be protected against imprisonment without cause and their right to a speedy trial. Lincoln did this as a war measure.

NORTHERN ARMIES FINALLY OVERPOWERED THE SOUTH

Southerners were making a heroic struggle, but the tide turned against them in the summer of 1863. From Virginia

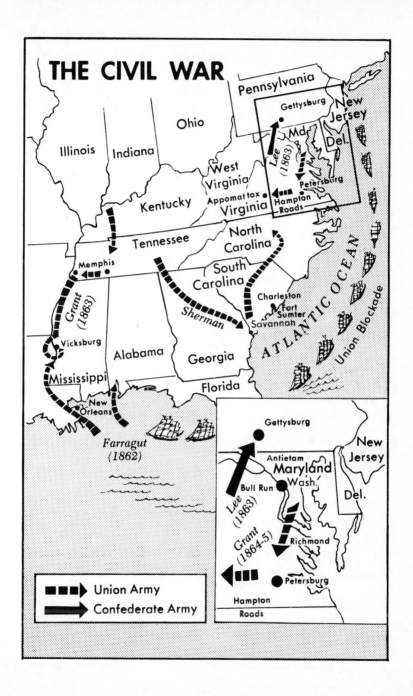

General Lee marched his army across Maryland and into Pennsylvania. A northern army commanded by General George Meade finally stopped him at Gettysburg. After a famous three-day battle, Lee was forced to retreat.

In the West, on the same day, General Grant's Union Army captured Vicksburg. This opened the Mississippi River for northern commerce all the way to New Orleans. It also cut off Texas and Arkansas from the rest of the South. Later in the summer, Confederate forces were driven from Lookout Mountain in eastern Tennessee. Chattanooga became a safe base for the Union Army. The North's next goal was Atlanta, Georgia.

Grant and Sherman Hammered at the Confederacy

General William T. Sherman took command of the Union forces in Tennessee, and Grant went east to take charge in Virginia.

In 1864 the Union intended to wear out the Confederate armies and break the South's power to resist. General Grant and General Lee fought some of the bloodiest battles of the war. In the long Battle of the Wilderness, at Spotsylvania Court House and at Cold Harbor, Grant lost thousands of men. But Lee's army was weakened too. Late in the summer Grant was outside Petersburg, not far from Richmond.

Meanwhile, General Sherman's army moved south from Chattanooga. By September, Sherman's army had captured Atlanta. Atlanta, a railroad center with many factories, was important to the South. General Sherman's armies burned down factories and public buildings and destroyed the railroad lines. As Sherman said, "War is hell."

From Atlanta, Sherman's army marched across Georgia to the seacoast at Savannah. The army lived off the countryside and destroyed everything—railroads, barns, animals, crops and factories—within a strip of land fifty miles wide. General Lee's army in Virginia could no longer obtain any supplies from Georgia or Alabama. The war was nearly over.

The War Ended at Appomattox

Early in 1865 General Lee's army was exhausted. His soldiers did not have enough guns, food or clothing. Many of them had given up and gone home. When Grant's army captured Petersburg, Lee turned west. Finally, near Appomattox Court House in April of 1865, Lee had to surrender.

One month later, the remaining Confederate armies also surrendered. The long war was over. Grant's terms for surrender were generous. Once in the West when he attacked a Confederate fort, Grant had demanded "unconditional surrender." People called him "Unconditional Surrender Grant." But this time Lee's soldiers were allowed to return to their homes. They could take their horses with them— "for the spring plowing," said Grant.

REVIEW ACTIVITIES

1. When war began, the North had many advantages. What were some of them?
2. Why was the South able to hold out for so long?
3. What was the Emancipation Proclamation? Did it settle the question of slavery?
4. Why were the battles of Gettysburg and Vicksburg so significant?
5. How did Sherman's "march to the sea" help to end the war?

Select the words that best complete the following sentences. (*Please do not write in this book.*)

1. The first battle of the war was fought at _____ _____ in the harbor of _____, South Carolina.

2. In 1862 the Confederate ship, the ——————, and the Union ship, the ————, battled at Hampton Roads.
3. The two most famous generals of the Civil War were ———— and ————.
4. To pay for the war, the federal government printed —— ———— and raised ————.
5. General ———— finally was forced to surrender near ———— Court House.

Who or what were the following:

1. George B. McClellan
2. John Pope
3. The draft
4. National Banking Act of 1863
5. George Meade

CHAPTER **11**

Reconstruction

THE SOUTH HAD TO REBUILD

When the War Between the States ended in 1865, the South was in ruins. Northern forces had torn up miles of southern railroad track. Many freight cars, stations, and factories had been destroyed. Confederate soldiers returned home to find their farms overgrown with weeds. Half of the South's cattle and horses were gone. Confederate money was worthless, and it was difficult to make a living. Jobs were very scarce.

In addition, defeat brought great changes in the usual pattern of southern life. Lincoln's Emancipation Proclamation had freed the slaves in the seceded states. But the Negroes were not used to freedom. Before the war, they had depended upon their owners for their room and board. Now landowners had lost their savings, and they had no cash to pay wages. Many former slaves had no place to live, no way to earn money and no education. Some stayed where they were and worked for their former masters; others wandered about in search of jobs.

Southern governments could do little to improve the situation. The Confederacy had fallen apart and the state governments had collapsed. Southerners who had fought for the Confederacy were no longer citizens. The only real authority in the South was the Union Army.

In short, the South had to rebuild nearly everything. Local government had to be restored. States had to be readmitted to the Union. Farms, businesses and railways had to be repaired. Former Confederate soldiers had to regain their citizenship. Former slaves had to find jobs and a way to live in freedom. All of this rebuilding was known as *reconstruction.*

Lincoln Hoped to Readmit the Southern States Quickly

President Lincoln had begun the work of reconstruction before the end of the war. In 1863 he promised a pardon to any Southerner who would take an oath of allegiance to the Union. After ten per cent of the voters in any state had taken this oath, said Lincoln, the state could form a new government. This was called Lincoln's "ten-per-cent plan." He intended to use this plan to bring all of the southern states back into the Union as quickly as possible.

Lincoln was re-elected President in 1864. In March of 1865 he was inaugurated for his second term. At that time he said, "With malice toward none, with charity for all, with firmness in the right as God gives us to see the right, let us strive on to finish the work we are in, to bind up the nation's wounds, to care for him who shall have borne the battle, and for his widow, and his orphan, to do all which may achieve and cherish a just and lasting peace among ourselves and with all nations." But Lincoln did not live to help "bind up the nation's wounds." One night in

April—only five days after Lee had surrendered—Lincoln was assassinated.

After Lincoln's death, Vice-President Andrew Johnson became the President. Johnson tried to carry out Lincoln's program. He urged the former Confederate states to follow Lincoln's "ten-per-cent plan." The South agreed and began to fulfill the terms. Southerners organized new governments and freed the slaves. They canceled southern war debts. They voted for the Thirteenth Amendment which Congress had proposed to end slavery. Soon the southern states were ready to rejoin the Union, and President Johnson was ready to take them back in. However, there were many radical Republicans in Congress who did not feel as Johnson did. These congressmen decided to oppose Johnson's policies.

Congress Wished to Punish the South

Congress met in December, 1865. The leaders of Congress were northern Republicans. They did not wish to follow Lincoln's plan for reconstruction. Instead the Republican leaders in Congress wanted to set up their own plan. They had three reasons for this. First, they wanted to continue the Republican Party's policies. They wanted to keep a high tariff. And they wanted to keep on giving away public lands to railways, speculators and western settlers. But they were afraid that the Southerners who had been elected to Congress under Lincoln's plan would not agree with them. The Southerners were all Democrats. So the Republican leaders refused to let them take their seats.

Second, many Northerners did not think that the South was being fair to the former slaves. They wanted to see to it that Negroes were treated as free men and that they were given their rights. Third, many northern radicals wanted revenge. They believed that the South should be punished for having caused the war. They wanted to "get tough" with the South.

The South, meanwhile, faced a big problem: What should

be the position of the former slaves? Almost none of them had any education. They could not learn all at once to be "responsible citizens." So no southern state gave Negroes the right to vote. And many states passed harsh laws with severe punishments for Negroes. Such laws came to be called "black codes." Republicans in Congress felt that states with such codes should not be allowed in the Union. They drew up their own plan for reconstruction. To help and protect Negroes in the South, Congress had already set up the Freedman's Bureau in 1865. The next year Congress gave the Freedman's Bureau more money and power to try law cases against Negroes in special courts.

In 1868 Congress passed the Fourteenth Amendment to the Constitution. This Amendment said that Negroes were to become citizens. It also declared that anyone who had sworn to uphold the Constitution and then fought against the Union would not be allowed to vote or hold office. This prevented most former southern leaders from taking a part in the government.

In 1867 Congress passed the First Reconstruction Act. This act put the South under military rule. The southern states were divided into five military districts with a United States Army officer in charge of each district. The Act also set down new conditions under which the seceded states could come back into the Union. The states had to ratify the Fourteenth Amendment and give Negroes the right to vote. President Johnson thought that these measures were too harsh. He vetoed the Reconstruction Act, but Congress passed the Act over his veto.

CONGRESS TRIED TO REMOVE JOHNSON FROM OFFICE

The congressional leaders were bitter because Johnson opposed them. They wanted to make sure that the President would keep Republicans in office and put their plans into effect. In March of 1867 Congress passed the Tenure of Office Act. This Act said that the President could not remove an appointed officeholder without the consent of the Senate. Several months later, Johnson played into the hands of his enemies. He dismissed Secretary of War Edwin Stanton who sided with radical Republicans. Johnson did this without the approval of the Senate.

So for the first and only time in our history, Congress attempted to remove the President from office. The House of Representatives passed an impeachment resolution. President Johnson was tried before the Senate. After eight weeks the senators gave their verdict. The vote fell one short of the two-thirds majority needed to remove the President. Johnson remained in office. However, the Republicans in Congress did not want Johnson to be re-elected. They wanted a man who would favor their policies.

In the presidential election of 1868, the Republicans nominated Ulysses S. Grant, a war hero. Of course the southern states would not vote for Grant. They resented the Republican reconstruction policies and favored the Democrats. But most of the southern states had not yet returned to the Union. Thus the Republicans won the election easily, and Grant became the President.

One by one the southern states did everything that Congress had demanded. Then, just to make sure, Congress proposed a new amendment in 1869. The Fifteenth Amendment said that no citizen could be denied the right to vote because of his race or his color, or because he had been a slave. The southern states accepted this Amendment too. By 1870 they were all back in the Union.

INEXPERIENCED MEN ROSE TO POWER IN THE SOUTH

The new state governments in the South pleased the Republicans. These governments did not represent the old southern white leaders. Former Confederate officers and government officials were not allowed to vote or hold office. So a new group of officials rose to power. Some of these men were white Southerners who had not fought in the war. They were called *scalawags*. Others were Negroes only recently freed from slavery. Still others were Northerners who went south after the war. Southerners called those people *carpetbaggers* because they frequently carried their belongings in bags made of cloth which looked like carpet.

Many of the new southern officials had little or no experience in running a government. Yet they were in charge of rebuilding the South. They raised taxes to repair war damage, rebuild railways and factories, put livestock back on the farms, and build schools for both Negro and white children. They did all this with too little care for expense. Often they spent money foolishly. A number of the carpetbaggers and scalawags misused their offices and made money for themselves dishonestly.

Although Southerners in general resented this corruption, they had no legal means to fight it. Therefore some of them adopted illegal methods. They joined secret societies such as the Ku Klux Klan. The Klan grew rapidly in the southern states. Its members wore white hoods and rode about the countryside at night to frighten carpetbaggers, scalawags and Negroes. Sometimes they resorted to violence, and sometimes, even murder. As a rule, only the most irresponsible white men joined the Klan. Decent Southerners opposed this organization. When Klan violence got out of control, federal soldiers were again sent to some districts.

After a while, the federal government began to relax its controls in the South. Many Northerners felt that the South had been punished enough. In 1872 when Grant was elected President for a second term, Congress passed a law that allowed most white Southerners to vote again. Gradually the South began to win back control of its own affairs.

When it was time for the election of 1876, the Democrats hoped to win for the first time since the Civil War. Carpetbag governments remained in only three southern states. Elsewhere, white Southerners would vote for the Democrats. There had been scandals and a depression, which you will read about in the next chapter. Democrats hoped that these events would persuade people to vote for their party. They named Samuel A. Tilden of New York as their candidate. The Republicans nominated Rutherford B. Hayes of Ohio.

In the election more people voted for Tilden than for Hayes. Thus Tilden won the *popular* vote. But this did not guarantee him victory. He did not have a majority of the *electoral* vote. There was a dispute over votes in the three "carpetbag" states of South Carolina, Louisiana and Florida. The Republicans and the Democrats both claimed victory in these states. As a result, each state sent two sets of election returns to Congress.

Congress had to decide which set of election returns should be accepted. Should they accept the Republican returns and give the election to Hayes? Or should they accept the Democratic returns and concede Tilden's election? Congress decided now to settle the question by appointing a special commission to count the votes. Eight members of the commission were Republicans and seven were Democrats. So the commission voted eight to seven in favor of the Republican candidate in all three states. This meant that Hayes now had more electoral votes than Tilden. Tilden refused to object, and Hayes became the President.

After the close election of 1876, the Republicans could not afford to be stern with the South much longer. In 1877 President Hayes called back all federal troops from the southern states. Before very long, the last three Republican governments in the South were voted out of office and the reconstruction period was ended.

THE SOUTH'S ECONOMY CHANGED

During the years following reconstruction, the South began to change. The free Negroes found a place in the economy. Though they were citizens, they were seldom allowed to vote, and they were "segregated" in schools and public places. Most of the large plantations were divided into small farms. Cotton was still important, but farmers began to plant other crops as well. In several states, tobacco-growing became very profitable. Southerners began to cut into their forests to supply the country with lumber. Factories for weaving cloth sprang up near the cotton fields. The discovery of oil in the Southwest brought increased prosperity to that area. The "new" South carved an important place for itself in the nation's economy.

However, Southerners did not forget the hardships of the reconstruction era. They blamed the northern Republicans for many of their difficulties. The South began voting solidly for Democratic candidates in election after election. This voting pattern continued for over fifty years, and the area became known as the *Solid South*.

REVIEW ACTIVITIES

1. Why was reconstruction necessary in the South after the Civil War?
2. What was Lincoln's ten-per-cent plan? What group opposed it? Why?
3. Why were impeachment proceedings brought against President Johnson? What was the outcome?
4. What was the purpose of the Fourteenth Amendment?

What was the purpose of the Fifteenth Amendment?
5. Describe the dispute caused by the election of 1876. How was this dispute settled?

Select the words that best complete the following sentences. (*Please do not write in this book.*)

1. After the war, the only real authority in the South was the _____ _____. During the reconstruction period, some white Southerners joined illegal societies like the ____ ____ ____.
2. Lincoln's _____ _____ freed the slaves in the _____ states.
3. _____ _____ became President after Lincoln's assassination. He _____ Lincoln's plan for reconstruction.
4. The _____ of _____ Act said that the President could not remove an appointed officeholder without the _____ consent.
5. After the period of reconstruction, the _____ began voting for the _____ Party in election after election.

Who or what were the following:

1. Scalawags
2. Carpetbaggers
3. "Black Codes"

4. Samuel Tilden
5. Rutherford B. Hayes

CHAPTER 12

America Becomes
a Nation of Industry

INDUSTRIALIZATION CREATED NEW PROBLEMS

During the period of southern reconstruction, the United States entered a new era—the age of machines. America gradually ceased to be a nation of small farmers, tradesmen and frontiersmen. Machines began to change the nature of life and work, both on the farms and in the factories. The population grew rapidly. More and more people began to live in cities and work for wages. Business companies became big, rich, and powerful. America was becoming "industrialized."

Growth and industrialization brought new problems to the nation. Farmers, small tradesmen and frontiersmen wanted little direct help from the government. For the most part, they wanted to be let alone. But industry wanted the government to protect it from foreign competition. Railways wanted free land and special favors. Should the government help to develop business and industry? Should big business companies be allowed to grow bigger? If so, how much bigger? If government helped business, what about the men and women who worked for wages in industry and on the railways? Should the government help them too? And, if the government helped the railways, should it also help the farmers?

As the country grew, so did the government. Mere size became a problem. Could a big government be efficient? Would all the officials be honest? Could a big government still be democratic?

The answers to these questions did not become clear to the American people all at once. How they arose, and what Americans did about them, will be told in the next chapters.

THE FRONTIER DISAPPEARED

The western half of the United States was settled between 1860 and 1890. From the Missouri River to the Pacific Coast, mountain lands and prairies began to fill up with farms, mining camps and cities. Before the Civil War, new gold and silver mines were discovered in Colorado and Nevada. More than 100,000 fortune hunters headed for Colorado in 1859 alone. And so many miners went to Nevada during the war that it became a new state in 1864. Mining towns grew up overnight. The gold and silver that they produced furnished the country with plenty of hard cash. This money helped the nation to prosper.

Railroads Helped to Link the West with the East

However, the Far West was separated from the rest of the country by mountains and dry plains. This made it difficult for people to send goods or letters back and forth across the country. For a while the mail was carried by riders on horseback. But this method was too slow. It took ten days for a letter mailed in St. Louis to reach California. Then telegraph wires were strung all the way to San Francisco. Eventually railroads were built to link the West with the East. It was the railroads that brought people and prosperity to the plains and mountain area.

The national government contributed a great deal to the growth of railroads. During the Civil War, Congress voted to give railroad companies some of the land owned by the government. Two companies were given the right to build a railroad line from Chicago to San Francisco. Congress gave each company ten square miles of land for every mile of track they built. Two years later the amount of land was doubled. The Union Pacific built its railway westward through Nebraska and over the mountains. The Central Pacific started at San Francisco and built eastward. They raced to see which company could put down the most track. In May of 1869 the two railroads met in Utah.

The federal government and the states gave land to other railways as well. Within twenty years there were four more routes to the Pacific. In 1860 there had been 30,000 miles of railway track. By 1890 there were 166,000 miles of track. These railways cost great sums of money. Without government aid, they could not have been built so quickly.

The railways did much for the West's economy. The first Westerners to benefit were those who raised cattle. These men let their cattle feed on open, public lands where there were no fences. Each animal wore its owner's brand. Every year cattlemen gathered large herds together and drove them across the prairies to Abilene, Dodge City or some other cow town on the railroad. From there the cattle were shipped to markets in the East.

The Homestead Act Encouraged Western Settlement

The government also helped to develop farms in the West. In 1862 Congress passed the Homestead Act which said that any man over 21 years of age could settle 160 acres of public land. If he lived on the land for five years and built a house on it, the land would then become his. A few years later, men in Kansas found that wheat would grow on the prairie. After that, thousands of settlers moved west and took up farming on free land. To protect their land, they enclosed it with barbed wire fences. Any other type of fence would have been too costly, but barbed wire had just been invented in the East. Fences kept the cattle from trampling the grain and eating it. The cattlemen did not like this, and they tried to stop farmers from building fences. But the farmers won in the end, partly because they were becoming more numerous, and partly because the cattle had already run out of good grazing land.

New Machinery Helped the Farmers

Between 1870 and 1880 Westerners settled nearly 96 million acres of new land. This created a need for improved farm machinery. In 1878 a man invented a machine that could cut and tie up grain in one operation. Seven years later an even better machine was invented. This one could cut the grain and then thresh it. As a result, farmers soon were raising more grain than they could sell. One farmer in 1890 could grow twenty times as much wheat as he could have grown forty years earlier. Thus the price of wheat fell very rapidly.

Prices for grain and meat remained low for many years. Farmers wanted the government to help raise prices by coining more money. They also wanted the government to make the railroads charge lower rates. They had little success, as you will see in the next chapter. Meanwhile, farm families continued to settle in the West. Montana, Washington, North Dakota and South Dakota became states in 1889. Idaho and Wyoming entered the Union in 1890. The West was no longer a "frontier."

During the Civil War the armed forces created a great demand for factory-made goods. Factory owners earned huge profits. After the war this prosperity continued. Railroad building kept many factories busy. New industries appeared and new machines were invented. New products came into use. The United States became a country with large and booming industries.

American industry was given a tremendous boost when an Englishman named Bessemer discovered a new way to make steel. The Bessemer process was introduced in the United States during the Civil War. After that, steel became almost as cheap as iron. It was much lighter and much stronger than iron. Steel replaced iron and wood in railway engines, cars and tracks. It was used to build machines for mills and factories all over the nation. Steel also made possible other machines—like the typewriter and the sewing machine—that were too bulky when made of iron or wood. Steel making became one of America's biggest industries.

Oil was another new industry. It was discovered in Pennsylvania in 1859. Soon kerosene, an oil product, replaced vegetable fats and whale oil for lighting houses and oiling machines. Gasoline engines began to replace bulky steam engines. Before the end of the century, automobiles were being built.

During the same years, electricity became a big business. The telegraph, invented in 1844, used electricity to send messages by wire. Telegraph companies covered the nation with a network of lines. In 1876 Alexander Graham Bell invented the telephone. Then electric power plants began to send power by wire to run machines. By 1879 Thomas A. Edison had invented a good electric light, and his company was selling electricity to light homes and factories in New York City.

Meat packing and food canning became big businesses during the Civil War. After the war these industries continued to grow. In 1875 the G. F. Swift meat company began using refrigerated railroad cars to ship fresh meat over long distances. Meanwhile, the nation's growing population provided industry with plenty of customers. The government helped, too, mostly by "protecting" industry from foreign competition.

The Government Protected American Business

You will remember that the Republican Party appealed to three main groups of people to elect President Lincoln in 1860. One group included those who were against slavery, and another group included those who wanted free land for farmers. Slavery was ended after reconstruction, and the Homestead Act provided free land for farmers. This left the third group. These included the northern factory owners who wanted a high tariff and bankers who wanted "sound" money.

In 1861 Congress had passed a high protective tariff. Since this occurred during the Civil War, there were no Southerners in Congress to vote against it. The tariff put a high tax on goods made in foreign countries and gave American factory owners an advantage. American manufacturers could charge high prices and make big profits without fear of foreign competition. Of course such a tariff meant that farmers and wage earners had to pay higher prices for the goods they needed. The Republicans believed that it was for the good of the country to make sure that industry prospered. So the tariff was not lowered. In fact, the Republicans passed higher tariffs in 1890 and again in 1897.

Greenbacks printed during the Civil War remained in use, but the government tried to keep them sound. After the war, the government started to take greenbacks out of circulation gradually. But with less money available, prices fell. This was particularly hard on farmers, many of whom were in debt. Complaints of hard times made the government stop calling in the greenbacks; in fact, during Grant's term, the number was somewhat increased again.

With a protective tariff and sound money, industry grew rapidly. In fact it grew too rapidly. Banks lent too much money. Many companies could not pay back their loans because business was not as good as they had expected. Several large banks had to close their doors. Many railroad owners, merchants, industrialists and storekeepers went bankrupt. When companies failed, men were put out of work; and the people who owned the bankrupt companies lost their savings. Prices went down. People who owed money, like the farmers, had a hard time paying off their debts. Business picked up again in a few years—but the farmers had to wait a long time for their prosperity.

COMPETITION LED TO MONOPOLY

By and large, American industry prospered during the years between 1865 and 1900 under the *free enterprise* system. Under this system any man who wished to do so was free to start any business. All he really needed was money, or backers with money, and the necessary "drive" to see his project through. Of course he also needed a bit of luck. But ambitious Americans believed in making their own luck and finding their own opportunities.

Business activity in the United States was also based on *competition*. When two men made the same product, their companies had to compete with one another. Each company tried to be efficient. Each one tried to sell its product for a lower price than the other. Thus, for as long as the competition lasted, buyers were able to get products of high quality at low prices.

That was the way the American system of free enterprise and competition was supposed to work. But the system did not always produce the best possible results. Sometimes one company managed to undersell all of its competitors. If the other companies in the same field could not match these low prices, they were driven out of business. When this happened, the competition was ended and the successful company had a *monopoly*. It could then charge whatever prices it wanted. The public had to pay these prices because it could not buy the products elsewhere. Since monopolies were very profitable, many businessmen tried to create them. They did this in several ways.

Frequently, one company bought up a competing company and added it to its own operation. In some cases two competing companies would join together and form one new company. This is called a *merger*. In other cases two or more companies would reduce competition by arranging to charge the same prices. They would agree to divide the market between them, or share their profits. An agreement to share profits is called a *pool*. On occasion, all the companies in one field formed a new super-company. The new super-company would manage all the others so that there would be no competition. Such an organization is called a *trust*.

Monopolies Were Set Up in the Oil and Steel Industries

One man who managed to develop a near monopoly was a young Scottish immigrant named Andrew Carnegie. Shortly after the Civil War, Carnegie built a mill in Pittsburgh and began to use the new Bessemer process for making steel. After a while he bought mines in Michigan to supply his own iron ore, and he built boats to ship his ore on the Great Lakes. Next Carnegie built a railroad from Lake Erie to Pittsburgh. Then he bought coal mines and began to make the coke needed for his steel mill. Finally he merged his vast holdings with the biggest coal and coke company in

Pittsburgh to form the Carnegie Steel Corporation. Carnegie Steel became so huge and so efficient that it had an advantage over all competitors.

The most famous monopoly of all occurred in the oil industry. Before crude oil from the ground can be used, it must be refined. That is, the impurities must be removed so that the oil can be made into a useful product, such as gasoline or kerosene. Soon after the Civil War, a young Cleveland merchant named John D. Rockefeller went into the oil refining business. Rockefeller was a very clever businessman. By cutting his own prices, he forced many competing refineries to close down. Then he bought up those refineries at low prices. He persuaded the railroads to charge him less for shipping oil than they charged the other refiners. The railroads were willing to do this because Rockefeller could give them a great deal of business. After a while Rockefeller was able to buy his own railroads, pipelines and storage plants. This cut his costs even further. Finally in 1870 he organized the Standard Oil Company, which controlled 90 per cent of the oil business in the country. Owners of oil wells had to sell to Standard Oil at Standard's own price. Users of oil had to pay whatever price the trust set.

Congress Passed the First Antitrust Act

Oil and steel were not the only industries to become monopolized. Trusts soon appeared in many other fields as well. When properly managed, these large business combinations frequently were very efficient. However, they gave a few businessmen a great deal of control over prices and over other businessmen. Eventually consumers began to complain. So the government decided to step in and regulate business in the public interest.

In 1890 Congress passed the Sherman Antitrust Act. This Act said that if a business combination prevented competition, it was illegal. The Act stated further that no one could combine to restrain trade or create a monopoly. Thus the largest business combinations were illegal. Congress passed the Sherman Act by a large majority. But for many years businessmen got around the law by organizing holding companies. These were special organizations that bought up and "held" stock in other companies. They had the same effect as trusts, but they were not specifically prohibited by the Sherman Act.

Most of the men who built American industry were honest and sincere. But there were others who had little or no regard for the public interest. Some of these men used illegal means to get what they wanted. If they thought that a special law would help them, they bribed congressmen and state legislators to vote for it. They even "rigged" stock prices to take the money of innocent investors. They cared little for the worker or the consumer. They said that their business was to make money and build industry, not to worry about anybody else. In general they resented the government's efforts to control business. But they did not resent the tariff that protected them and the other laws that helped them to prosper.

CORRUPTION LED TO REFORM IN POLITICS

Just as there were abuses in business, so were there abuses in government. In fact, during the period following the Civil War, there seemed to be an overall letdown in moral standards. Such letdowns often come after wars.

Government officials and politicians accepted gifts from businessmen in return for favors. During the reconstruction period, state governments in the South were full of graft and corruption. And in New York "Boss" Tweed's city government was so bad that finally Tweed was put in jail. Many officials used their positions to get public money for themselves and their friends. For a time people seemed to forget the high ideals that they had held during the Civil War.

GRANT'S ADMINISTRATION WAS MARRED BY SCANDAL

Corruption in government was especially bad during the administration of President Grant. One famous scandal even involved a number of congressmen. After Congress had voted to give public lands to the Union Pacific Railway, a private company was formed to build the tracks. The company then charged the railroad nearly double what it cost to build the tracks. Some congressmen were made part owners of the company, and they took their share of the unfair profits.

Another scandal took place in the Treasury Department. A few dishonest treasury officials took bribes from whiskey manufacturers in return for not collecting the full tax on whiskey. When the story was discovered, the officials had to resign.

President Grant himself was involved in one case. Two speculators, Jay Gould and James Fisk, planned to make a profit by buying and selling gold. To make their plan work, they had to be sure that the government would not sell any of its gold. So they convinced President Grant that business would be helped if the government stopped selling gold. Then they bought up almost all the gold in the country and offered it for sale at a much higher price. Banks had to have gold to do business, but many of them could not afford to pay the high prices. They faced ruin. Finally President Grant realized what was going on, and he ordered the government to start selling gold again. The plan of the two speculators failed. President Grant himself did not profit from any of these crooked practices. However, many government jobs were still held by men who were corrupt, lazy, incompetent, or ignorant. This was partly due to the way in which government jobs were filled.

139

Ever since the time of Andrew Jackson, many government jobs had been filled by means of the spoils system. This meant that a political party would fill government posts with its own supporters. Each time a different party won an election, a new group of men took office.

As the nation grew, so did the government. Government services were expanded at every level. Some of these services could only be provided by trained people. But the political bosses often appointed government employees who had no experience or were even dishonest.

President Rutherford B. Hayes, Grant's successor, tried to pass reforms that would correct these abuses. But Hayes received little support. President Hayes was succeeded in office by James A. Garfield. Several months after he was sworn in, Garfield was shot by a disappointed office-seeker who had expected the President to give him a government job. This incident served to point out the failings of the spoils system. The public began to demand reform.

Reform came during the administration of Chester A. Arthur, the man who became the President when James Garfield died. In 1883 Congress passed the Pendleton Act which provided that certain government jobs would be permanent. Those who wanted these jobs would have to pass an examination. A Civil Service Commission would make up the examination, and the job would be given to the man with the highest grade. This man could keep his job regardless of which party won the next election. The President would decide which jobs would be covered by civil service regulations.

President Arthur placed about 14,000 jobs under the new civil service rules. Other Presidents have added to that number. Today more than eight out of ten government jobs are under civil service rules.

REVIEW ACTIVITIES

1. What problems did industrialization create for the nation?
2. How did the national and state governments contribute to the growth of railroads?
3. What was the Homestead Act?
4. What are some of the new industries that developed during and right after the Civil War?
5. American business grew under conditions of free competition. How did monopolies develop?

Select the words that best complete the following sentences. (*Please do not write in this book.*)

1. When two companies join together and form a new company this is known as a _____. An agreement between two or more companies to share profits is called a _____.
2. The _____ _____ Act said that any business combination that prevented _____ was illegal.
3. Corruption in government was especially bad during the administration of President _____. One famous scandal even involved a number of _____.
4. Ever since Andrew Jackson's administration many _____ jobs had been filled by means of the _____ _____.
5. The _____ Act provided that certain _____ jobs would be permanent regardless of which party won the next election.

Who or what were the following:

1. Alexander Graham Bell
2. Thomas A. Edison
3. Greenbacks
4. Andrew Carnegie
5. John D. Rockefeller

CHAPTER **13**

Areas of Discontent

LABOR UNIONS TRIED TO HELP WORKERS

In the years before 1900, the United States grew rapidly both in size and in wealth. But farmers and factory workers did not share in the prosperity created by big business. Corporations made large profits, but the men who worked in factories and on the railroads continued to receive low wages. And they had to work long hours. In the steel mills men worked twelve hours a day, six days a week. Women in stores worked from seven-thirty in the morning until nine at night. The average pay was two dollars a day. Workers could not save money for illness, accidents, old age or unemployment. They were never sure that they would be able to keep their jobs. They could not argue with their employers. The boss could always fire one worker and hire somebody else. Most employers did not worry about how their workers lived. The only way that the workers could improve their position was to band together to form labor unions.

Labor unions existed in the United States long before the Civil War. But most of the early unions were small and weak. Their members usually came from only one locality. The courts frequently opposed these unions when they tried to strike. Still the labor movement grew. Shortly before the war, several national unions were started. More were founded during and after the war. In 1866 several of these unions joined together to form the National Labor Union. The Union entered politics and tried to get new laws that would help workers. But it got little public support and fell apart during the 1870's.

The Knights of Labor Gave Way to the A.F. of L.

In 1869 another labor organization arose. It was called The Noble Order of the Knights of Labor. By 1886 the Knights of Labor claimed 700,000 members. The Knights worked for shorter hours and higher wages. They tried to run cooperative stores for their members, but these failed. The Knights also took part in a number of strikes, but these also failed. This combination of setbacks was too much for the organization. It declined rapidly, and after 1894 it was no longer important. By this time, however, there was another group to take its place.

In 1886 labor leaders organized the American Federation of Labor. The A.F. of L.'s President was Samuel Gompers, head of the Cigar Makers' Union. Gompers believed that labor unions should not go into politics. Labor's goals, said Gompers, should be higher wages, shorter hours and better working conditions. To get them, Gompers said unions should bargain with their employers, and, if necessary, strike.

Employers, however, were not used to talking about their business with the workers. They did not like to bargain over wages and often they refused to see the union leaders. So the unions had to go on strike. But strikes did not work well.

Employers merely hired new workers to take the place of those who went on strike. The public seldom took the side of the workers. The government usually sided with the employers. Nevertheless, the number of strikes increased. Three of these strikes are famous.

Violence Accompanied Several Strikes

First there was the great railroad strike of 1877. Men on the trains earned seven dollars a week. The depression that began in 1873 cut railroad profits, and the companies tried to save money by cutting wages. In 1877 the Baltimore and Ohio Railroad cut wages for the fourth time in seven years. The Ohio's workers went on strike and the strike spread to other railroads from New York to Texas. When the companies hired new men to run the trains, strikers overturned railroad cars in order to keep the trains from running. They ruined locomotives and destroyed buildings. The railroads asked the federal government to help them. The government agreed and sent soldiers to keep strikers away from the railroad tracks. The strike failed.

Perhaps the worst strike came in 1892 at the Carnegie Steel plant in Homestead, Pennsylvania. The plant wanted to cut wages. When the Iron and Steel Workers Union objected, the plant closed its doors and hired 300 detectives to keep the workers out. There was a battle with gunfire and the strikers drove the detectives out of town. Then the company asked the Governor of Pennsylvania for help. The governor sent soldiers to Homestead and set up military law. Many people felt sorry for the strikers. But when a man tried to murder the manager of the Homestead plant, people turned against the strikers. The strikers had to give up. Most of the workers never got their jobs back. The union was broken.

Another big strike took place in 1894. It involved the Pullman Company which made sleeping cars and ran them on the railways. The company paid low wages. And it made the workers pay high rents to live in company houses. Workers also had to buy their goods in company stores that charged high prices. The strike began when the Pullman Company cut wages but did not reduce rents. To help the strikers at the Pullman plant, the American Railway Workers Union refused to move trains that had Pullman cars. Railroad companies began to lose money. They persuaded the President to send troops to Chicago to see that the trains would run. The excuse for the President's action was that the strike was interfering with the delivery of United States mail. The Attorney General got a court order, or *injunction,* that said workers could not interfere with the railroads. Several union members were arrested, and the strike failed.

Working Conditions Improved Very Slowly

In each of these big strikes, the federal government sided with employers. Few important people sided with the workers. Just the same, the American Federation of Labor continued to grow, and some of its strikes did succeed. Lawmakers gradually began to see that they should protect the welfare of the workers. In 1886 Massachusetts passed a law saying that factory owners could not hire children under ten years of age. Several states passed laws that made employers pay for accidents to their workers. In 1892 Congress set up an eight-hour day for all government workers. But such laws were not general. As late as 1905 a New York law that limited the hours of workers in bakeries was declared unconstitutional. It was years before organized labor was strong enough to get far in its demands against employers.

FARMERS FOUGHT RAILROADS

For many years after the Civil War, farmers had much to complain about. Farmers were producing more meat and grain than they could sell at good prices. They were not prosperous. They complained about the high interest rates they had to pay on the money they borrowed for land, machinery and livestock. Sometimes they paid 15 or even 20 per cent on loans. When they could not keep up these payments, the banks took over their property. Farmers also complained about high taxes. There was no income tax in those days. The main tax was on land. Farmers argued that their taxes were far higher than the taxes of the businessman. In addition, they complained about the high prices of manufactured goods and railroad freight.

The only way a farmer could get his wheat to market was on the railroad. He had to pay whatever the railroad wanted to charge him. Sometimes the railroad asked him for 20 cents to carry one bushel of grain for 200 miles.

Many Farmers Joined the Grange

Individual farmers could do little by themselves. Therefore some of them formed a society called The Patrons of Husbandry. Each branch of this society was called a "grange," and the society soon became known simply as the Grange. The Grange got farmers to sell and ship their grain together. Then it went to state legislatures and demanded that laws be passed to control the railroads. In 1869 the Illinois Legislature passed a law that made railroads charge the same rates to everyone. Two years later the same legislature passed another law that stated exactly how much railroads could charge for storing and shipping grain. Most states in the Middle West followed the example of Illinois.

Railroad officials said that these Granger Laws, as they were called, took away their right to make a profit. They tried to have the laws declared unconstitutional. But for a long time the Granger Laws were upheld by the courts. In 1876 the Supreme Court decided in one case that states could control railway prices "for the common good." Then the state legislatures that were controlled by farmers began to put railroad prices still lower. The railroads complained. Finally the Supreme Court made a new decision. In 1886 the Court said that the states could not reduce railroad rates to a point where they prevented railroads from making a profit. At the same time, the Supreme Court said that railroads were engaged in interstate commerce if they crossed state lines. Since the states had no control over interstate commerce, the farmers had to appeal to Congress. There they received support from others.

Congress Passed the Interstate Commerce Act

Farmers were not the only ones who suffered from high and uneven railroad rates. Businessmen also complained. Railroads had formed pools to keep their prices high. They would give low rates to powerful men such as Carnegie or Rockefeller but high rates to men who owned smaller companies. Sometimes railroads would hand back or "rebate" part of the freight costs to a big company. Sometimes a railroad charged more to send freight on a "short haul" of 40 miles than to send the same amount of freight on a "long haul" from Chicago to New York where there was competition from other railroads. So, many businessmen joined the farmers in demanding that Congress control the railroads.

In 1887 Congress met these demands by passing the Interstate Commerce Act. This act said: 1) railroad rates had to be fair and the same for all—no special rates or rebates were to be allowed; 2) railroad pools were prohibited; and 3) it was illegal to charge more for a short haul than for a long one.

An Interstate Commerce Commission was set up to enforce these rules. For many years railroads found ways to get around the Interstate Commerce Commission. Later the Commission was given more power and the worst of the railroad abuses were ended.

Farmers had to buy clothes and tools from factories. Because of high tariffs, American factories could charge high prices. Farmers, in general, wanted tariffs to be lowered.

Nearly every farmer who settled in the West borrowed money to pay for his land, his animals and his tools. He was in debt. If agricultural prices went down, he could not make enough money to pay off his debts. If prices went up, he could sell his crops for more money and pay back the money he had borrowed from the bank.

Unfortunately for the farmers, agricultural prices did go down in the depression of 1873. And they did not go back up after the depression. Therefore, the farmers wanted the government to do something to raise prices. They wanted the government to issue more money. If there were more money, people could afford to buy more agricultural products. Prices would go up and the farmers could pay their debts. In short, the farmers wanted a little inflation.

Bankers and businessmen, on the other hand, did not want inflation. They wanted sound money that would keep its value. Thus they opposed the farmers and argued that the government should not increase the amount of money in circulation. This argument reached its high point during the exciting election of 1896.

The United States Began to Coin Silver Money

You will remember that the federal government issued paper money, or greenbacks, during the Civil War. After the war the government started to redeem (buy back) these greenbacks to take them out of circulation. This action reduced the amount of money in circulation. But congressmen from farm states objected, and the government had to stop redeeming the greenbacks. This helped the farmers some, but they still wanted more and cheaper money. So they urged the government to resume coining silver dollars. The government had stopped buying silver to put in coins after the California Gold Rush of 1849.

The owners of silver mines in Nevada and Colorado agreed with the farmers. These mine owners also wanted the government to buy and coin silver. Together the farmers and miners finally persuaded Congress to act.

In 1878 Congress made silver a part of the United States money system. The Bland-Allison Act stated that the Treasury was to buy and coin between 2 and 4 million dollars worth of silver each month. This act helped the farmers a bit, but it was opposed by businessmen.

The Democrats Won the Election of 1884 but Lost in 1888

When the election of 1884 came, the Republican Party would have nothing to do with President Arthur because he stood up to the party bosses and approved of civil service. The Republicans nominated James G. Blaine of Maine. The Democrats chose Grover Cleveland, the Governor of New York. For the first time since Lincoln was elected, the Democrats won enough northern votes to carry the election, and Cleveland became the President.

Several of Cleveland's policies displeased groups with special interests. For example, the politicians did not like Cleveland because he approved of civil service reform and put about 7,000 more jobs under civil service rules. Veterans did not like him because he vetoed their pension bills. Big business did not like him because he tried unsuccessfully to reduce the tariffs. And farmers were unhappy because Cleveland did not coin as many silver dollars as he was allowed to make. As a result, the Republicans won the election of 1888 and General Benjamin Harrison of Indiana became the next President.

During Harrison's administration the Republicans drew up a new tariff bill named after Senator McKinley. The new

McKinley Bill raised the rates on manufactured goods higher than they had ever been. It also raised tariff rates on farm products. Republicans claimed that this would bring higher prices for farm goods. They said that the farmers would prosper. But congressmen from farm states did not want a high tariff. They felt that coining more silver would do the farmers more good than a higher tariff on farm products. They agreed to vote for the McKinley Bill only if Congress would provide for more silver dollars. So, in 1890, Congress passed the Sherman Silver Purchase Act that doubled the number of silver dollars the government was required to make. Then western congressmen voted for the McKinley Tariff Bill. But farm prices continued to fall.

Feeling that a change would help them, the farmers started a campaign to vote Republicans out of office in the election of 1890. And the farmers were very successful. In the next House of Representatives there were only 88 Republicans. By contrast, the Democrats held 244 seats.

The Populist Party Was Founded

Some farmers thought that neither of the existing political parties would help them. So they formed their own third party and called themselves the *Populists*. Populists demanded cheap loans to farmers. They called for an income tax that would make businessmen pay a larger share of government expenses. They wanted the government to own and run the railroads. They also wanted United States senators to be elected by the people, not by state legislatures. Most of all, they wanted the government to be able to coin an unlimited amount of silver dollars.

In the election of 1892, the Populists received a large number of votes, but not enough to win the election. The Democrats had renominated Grover Cleveland. They opposed the McKinley Tariff Bill and they won the election. Cleveland was elected, and for the first time since the Civil

War, the Democrats had a majority in both houses of Congress. Would the Democrats pass laws to help the farmers?

CLEVELAND FACED A SEVERE DEPRESSION

Soon after Cleveland moved into the White House, the country suffered another depression. Farm prices became so low farmers could not pay off their debts. Banks failed. Factories could not sell their goods, and many of them were forced to close. Workers lost their jobs. For a time one man in five was out of work. An Ohio businessman named Jacob Coxey led a march of unemployed workers to Washington to demand a program of public works that would give men jobs. But Congress would not listen to them.

Cleveland was worried mostly about the value of money. The federal government was receiving less money from taxes. But it still had to buy up silver and pay for it in gold. Soon the government had very little gold left. Cleveland believed in sound money. He wanted American dollars to be backed by gold. He demanded repeal of the Silver Purchase Act. Congress repealed the law and the government stopped buying silver. Cleveland borrowed gold through the banking firm of J. P. Morgan. Money became sound. But the farmers felt that Cleveland had let them down.

Congress did little to help either the farmers or the unemployed. Cleveland persuaded Congress to reduce the tariff a little and let some goods come into the country without any tax at all. But tariff rates were still high. Congress also passed an income tax law. But the Supreme Court said that the law was unconstitutional. This was the situation on the eve of the national election in 1896.

Democrats Lost the Election of 1896

The election campaign of 1896 was very exciting. The country was not yet fully out of the depression, and many people were dissatisfied. Many groups wanted the government to take action.

Workers wanted jobs. They wanted laws to help them get better wages and shorter working hours. They were angry because the government always took the side of big business on the issue of strikes. Farmers were still troubled by debts and low prices. They wanted lower interest rates, stricter railroad controls and free coinage of silver. Many other people also wanted reforms. Reformers wanted the voters instead of the state legislatures to elect senators. They wanted to vote by secret ballot, and they wanted voters—as well as party leaders—to name candidates for office. Such reforms, they said, would make the government more democratic. Then the people could get what they wanted.

In 1896 angry reformers, farm leaders and friends of labor went to the Democratic Party Convention in Chicago. They took over the convention and turned their backs on President Cleveland. They made the Democratic Party stand for low tariffs, silver money, an income tax law that would remain and more action against big trusts. This platform favored labor, the farmers and reform. It did not favor big business.

At the height of the convention, a young lawyer from Nebraska made a famous speech. His name was William Jennings Bryan. His speech was in favor of silver dollars. The gold standard, said Bryan, was the cause of misery across the country. Amidst mounting excitement, Bryan concluded:

". . . We have petitioned, and our petitions have been scorned; we have entreated, and our entreaties have been disregarded; we have begged, and they have mocked when our calamity came. We beg no longer; we entreat no more; we petition no more. We defy them . . . We will answer their demand for a gold standard by saying to them: You shall not press down upon the brow of labor this crown of thorns; you shall not crucify mankind upon a cross of gold."

The Democrats made Bryan their candidate for President. So did the Populist Party.

The Republican Party chose Senator William McKinley of Ohio as their candidate. He had been the author of the McKinley Tariff Bill. The Republicans felt that free coinage of silver would ruin the nation's economy. It would make money worthless, they said, and it would cause people to lose their savings. The Republicans stood firmly for the gold standard, and they blamed the depression on the Democrats. The issues in this election were clear.

Bryan began a whirlwind campaign. A powerful orator, he made 600 speeches in 29 states. But Bryan had to do almost everything alone. The Democratic Party did not have money for other speakers. The Republicans, on the other hand, raised large sums of money to pay for their campaign. They sent speakers everywhere that Bryan went. They printed pamphlets, organized rallies and pictured Bryan as a dangerous radical.

The turnout at the polls on election day was the largest in our history up to that time. The country made its decision and chose McKinley. The farmers and reformers had lost.

MCKINLEY BROUGHT PROSPERITY BUT FEW REFORMS

McKinley's election meant that the government would be friendly to big business for four more years. McKinley did not believe in enforcing the laws against trusts. He also stood for sound money and a high tariff.

President McKinley called Congress into a special session to ask for a new tariff bill. In July of 1897 the Dingley Tariff became law. It made the taxes on imported goods higher than they had ever been before.

The Republicans also voted for sound currency. They passed the Gold Standard Act in 1900. It provided that all

United States money—paper bills or silver—could be exchanged for gold. Fortunately, this did not result in less money in circulation. New gold mines in Alaska and South Africa were discovered. They produced plenty of gold for all the world. Farm prices did not go down.

The number and size of trusts increased. Big bankers helped rival businesses to combine with one another. Manufacturers created larger and larger corporations. One of the largest was the United States Steel Corporation. This giant of industry was built by J. P. Morgan. Morgan gathered money from several sources. He bought the steel mills of Andrew Carnegie and joined them with others. The Sherman Antitrust Act did not disturb men like J. P. Morgan. Everyone felt sure that McKinley would not enforce the Act. People who wanted "reforms" had little power.

McKinley's Death Made Roosevelt President

In 1900 the Republican Party renominated McKinley as their presidential candidate. For Vice-President they chose Theodore Roosevelt, the Governor of New York.

Roosevelt represented the liberal element within the Republican Party. He was a "reform" governor. The political boss of New York State did not like Roosevelt's reforms. Because he wanted Roosevelt out of the way, he arranged to have Roosevelt named for the vice-presidency.

The Democratic Party again nominated William Jennings Bryan. The Democrats wanted to enforce the law against trusts, reduce the tariff and protect factory laborers.

But there was no real dissatisfaction in the country. Things were going well, and the Republicans won the election by a wide margin.

The politicians who controlled the Republican Party expected no trouble for four more years. However, they were disappointed. McKinley was assassinated by an anarchist in September, 1901. Theodore Roosevelt became President.

REVIEW ACTIVITIES

1. Why were labor unions formed? How successful were they before 1900?
2. Why did the farmers want the Granger Laws?
3. What was the Interstate Commerce Act? How effective was it?
4. Did the McKinley Tariff please the farmers? Explain your answer.
5. Why was the Populist Party founded? What did it stand for?

Select the words that best complete the following sentences. (*Please do not write in this book.*)

1. Samuel _____ was President of the American Federation of Labor. He believed that _____ _____ should not go into politics.
2. The _____ of Pennsylvania helped break the strike at the _____ Steel plant.
3. The _____ Party won the election of 1884 and _____ _____ became the President.
4. In the late 1800's farmers were in favor of _____ interest rates and the _____ _____ of silver.
5. The _____ _____ Act provided that all United States money could be exchanged for _____.

Who or what were the following:

1. Noble Order of the Knights of Labor
2. Samuel Gompers
3. J. P. Morgan
4. William McKinley
5. William Jennings Bryan

CHAPTER **14**

The Beginnings of Reform

ROOSEVELT OFFERED A SQUARE DEAL

Theodore Roosevelt became President of the United States after McKinley died in 1901. Roosevelt knew that big business was important to America, but he thought that business should be operated for the good of the people. Further, he believed that the government should help to protect the public interest. So Roosevelt began to enforce the Antitrust Act. Roosevelt's Attorney General brought a suit against the Northern Securities Corporation, one of the biggest of the trusts. Many men in the Republican Party complained about this, but the public supported Roosevelt. In 1904 the Supreme Court said that the men who founded the Northern Securities Corporation had violated the Sherman Antitrust Act. The next year, the Supreme Court declared that the beef trust was illegal. This trust included all of the big meat-packing companies. While Roosevelt was President, the government sued more than twenty big corporations. For this, Roosevelt was called a "trust buster."

Roosevelt also thought that the government should see to it that railroads operated for the good of the people. He urged Congress to strengthen the Interstate Commerce Act. As a result Congress passed new legislation dealing with rebates. It was already illegal for railroads to give rebates. Now it became illegal for businessmen to accept rebates. This change made it easier to enforce the law.

The railroads continued to be a problem. Railroads still set their own rates, and where they had no competition, the rates were high. In 1906 Congress gave the Interstate Commerce Commission power to decide what rates the railroads should charge. It also gave the Commission power to regulate express companies, sleeping car companies, and pipe lines.

Roosevelt's idea about the role of government involved him in settling a strike. In 1902 coal miners in eastern Pennsylvania went on strike. The mine operators refused to talk with the union leaders. They simply closed their mines, and no coal was taken out that summer. Had the strike continued, people in the eastern United States would have had no coal to heat their homes in the winter. Roosevelt urged union leaders and mine owners to think of the needs of the people. The union leaders agreed to let outside parties make recommendations, but the owners would not agree. Roosevelt had to do something. Other Presidents had used the army and the courts to help break a strike. Roosevelt put the pressure on mine owners. He talked about sending federal troops to seize the mines and run them. Since that was the last thing that the mine owners wanted to see happen, they agreed to accept the decision of a committee. In October the strikers went back to work. Roosevelt said he had tried to give a "square deal" to both sides in this dispute. Soon the term *Square Deal* was used to describe the entire program of reforms which Roosevelt had started.

Reforms Came During Roosevelt's Second Term

Although many party politicians and big businessmen did not approve of him, Roosevelt knew how to get the public on his side. In 1904 the party leaders again nominated him for President, and he was elected. He supported more reforms.

A favorite target of the reformers was the food and drug industry. Food and drugs were sold under false labels. Cans or bottles did not always contain what the labels said they did. Congress passed the Pure Food and Drug Act in 1906. This law required the manufacturer to show on the label exactly what was inside the package. The same year, Congress passed the Meat Inspection Act. This Act provided that all meat shipped across state borders must come from healthy animals, and that it must be prepared under clean and sanitary conditions. The Act also said that federal officers should see to it that the meat packers obeyed this law.

Roosevelt made it clear that big business could no longer operate without regard for other people. Trusts would not be allowed to stifle competition. Business owners could not count on the government to help them break strikes. Railways no longer were free to charge any rates they wanted. Food manufacturers were compelled by law to be clean and honest. Roosevelt insisted that the government had a right to interfere with business in order to protect public interest.

LOCAL GOVERNMENTS BECAME MORE DEMOCRATIC

While these reforms took place on the national level, political changes were made in the states and cities. Between the election of 1884 and the middle of the twentieth century, every state but South Carolina adopted the secret ballot. Up until that time, men marked their ballots in public.

Political bosses could see how everybody voted. If a party leader paid a man to vote one way, it was possible to check up and see if he had voted that way. The secret ballot helped to eliminate this practice.

Another step in election reform was to change the way parties chose candidates for public office. Nominating conventions had existed in this country since the early nineteenth century. But few party members could attend the conventions, and candidates actually were chosen by a few party leaders. To correct this, reformers began to demand a "direct primary" in which every party member could help choose his party's candidates. Wisconsin adopted the direct primary in 1903. A short time later, a number of states followed Wisconsin's lead.

Many states also adopted measures known as *Initiative, Referendum* and *Recall.* Initiative gives voters the right to begin legislation. If a certain number of voters—usually five to ten per cent—sign a petition asking for a new law, the state legislature must vote on it. Referendum enables the people to vote directly on any law that the legislature has passed or has refused to pass. Initiative and Referendum give the voting public a chance to keep the legislature on its toes. Recall gives the people the power to vote a man out of office before the end of his term. If an official or a legislator does not do what people expect and enough people demand an election, they vote on whether or not the man should remain in office. About half of the states adopted one or more of these democratic reforms, but they never became part of the United States Constitution.

TWO NEW AMENDMENTS WERE ADDED TO THE CONSTITUTION

For many years after the United States was established, women were not allowed to vote. When Wyoming became a state in 1890, however, women were given the right to vote in state elections. Colorado, Utah and Idaho followed Wyoming's lead. However, women did not get the right to vote in national elections until 1920 when the Nineteenth Amendment was added to the Constitution.

Another reform concerned the way we choose United States senators. The Constitution had given the state legislatures the power to elect senators. Senators chosen in this way did not always represent the people. Sometimes ambitious men could bribe enough state legislators to get elected. For many years, reformers wanted to have senators elected directly by the people. Finally, Congress proposed the Seventeenth Constitutional Amendment, and it was adopted in 1913. Since then each senator has been elected by all the voters in the state he represents.

TAFT CONTINUED MANY OF ROOSEVELT'S POLICIES

When President Roosevelt's term was over, he did not want to run again. The Republican Party nominated William Howard Taft, Roosevelt's Secretary of War. Taft won the election and became the President in 1909.

The Republicans had promised to change the tariff law and reduce some of the duties. But Congress actually increased as many duties as it reduced. Congress also proposed an amendment to the Constitution that would make an income tax legal.

Taft followed Roosevelt's policies dealing with railroads and trusts. He persuaded Congress to give the Interstate Commerce Commission more power. Congress gave the Commission the right to start lawsuits against the railroads. The Commission also was given the power to regulate telegraph companies. Taft's administration continued to check big trusts. Roosevelt had said that it was not the size of a trust but its purpose that made it dangerous. And Taft agreed.

He said there were good trusts and bad trusts. During his four years in office, Taft started more lawsuits against trusts than Roosevelt had in seven years. For instance, both the Standard Oil Company and the American Tobacco Company were forced to break up into separate companies.

WILSON OFFERED THE NEW FREEDOM

Despite these moves, some people demanded more reforms. They wanted better laws for controlling trusts, a much lower tariff, a more flexible money system and greater freedom for labor unions. The Democratic Party stood for these reforms, and the party was gaining strength. Roosevelt and his friends thought the Republican Party should favor some of these reforms too.

Before the election of 1912, Roosevelt and the liberals in the Republican Party split with the regular leaders. The regulars nominated Taft. So Roosevelt organized his own Progressive Party and ran for President once again. The Democrats nominated Governor Woodrow Wilson of New Jersey.

The Democrats promised lower tariffs, stronger laws against trusts and fair treatment for labor. Wilson did not want to do away with big business, but he was against monopoly. He said he wanted to give all business—big and small—an equal chance to compete for a share of the markets. He called his program *The New Freedom.*

In the election, some Republicans voted for Taft and some for Roosevelt. As a result, Wilson received more votes than either of them. He was elected President by a large majority in the Electoral College.

Wilson's first message to Congress was delivered in person. In order to carry out the reforms he had promised, Wilson asked Congress for speedy action. Most of his program was adopted quickly.

The New Freedom Was a Change in Emphasis

The New Freedom was more than a program of reforms. It was a change in emphasis. For years the emphasis in the national government had been on helping business to grow. The New Freedom emphasized the duty of the national government to help everybody. It emphasized the fact that some groups of people occasionally need to be protected against other groups of people. The New Freedom included plans to protect small businessmen against monopolies and to protect the consumer from high prices. It sought to protect laborers against unfair or selfish employers. And it sought to give everybody in the nation a better system of banking and money.

To protect the consumer from very high prices, Congress lowered the tariff. The Underwood Tariff Act, passed in 1913, made the first real reductions in the tariff laws since the Civil War. It permitted a number of articles to be imported free of tax.

Congress also passed an income tax law. This law was made constitutional by the Sixteenth Amendment. The Amendment was adopted in 1913. The income tax made people with high incomes pay more of the costs of government than people with low incomes. It protected the farmer and the average working man from having to pay too much in taxes.

Congress Passed New Laws to Control Business and Help Labor

To help control monopolies, Congress passed two laws that Wilson recommended. One law set up a Federal Trade Commission. Congress gave the Commission power to look into the operations of business firms. If it found that a firm was misrepresenting its product or otherwise breaking the law, it could order changes. If the firm ignored the order to change its practices, the Commission could take the case to the federal courts.

A second law dealing with monopolies was the Clayton Antitrust Act. The Clayton Act made it clear for the first time what kind of trusts and business combinations were to be considered unfair. For example, the law made it illegal for a businessman to run more than two big companies in the same line of business. It also closed the loopholes in previous antitrust legislation. One part of the Clayton Act helped labor unions. For the first time Congress declared that strikes and picketing were legal. The Clayton Act also said that the government could not break up a strike by jailing labor leaders without a trial.

Another act of Congress helped merchant seamen. The Seamen's Act, passed in 1915, required ship owners to provide good quarters, decent food and better working hours for sailors. In order to make ships safer, the law also required that ships meet certain standards.

Finally, Congress actually passed a law to help settle a labor dispute. You remember that twice before 1900 the federal government had helped to break up strikes on the railroads. Both times the government sent army troops to help the railway owners. Once the government obtained a court order that made it illegal to lead a railway strike. Under President Wilson, the government did something quite different.

In 1916 railroad owners and the labor unions had a dispute over wages and hours of work. When they could not reach an agreement, the unions threatened to strike. A nationwide railway strike would result in hardship and loss to everyone. Wilson urged Congress to act. He wanted power to settle the dispute for the good of the nation. He was not able to get that power. Instead Congress passed the Adamson Act that gave railway workers an eight-hour day with no cut in wages. By seeing to it that some of labor's demands were met by the employers, Congress helped to settle the strike.

The Federal Reserve Act Strenghtened the Nation's Banks

One of the most important reforms in Wilson's program set up a new banking system. Congress passed the Federal Reserve Act in 1913. The National Banking Act of 1863 had allowed national banks to issue their own money. This paper money was backed by government bonds. The money was sound, but the system did not work too well. There was always the same amount of money in circulation. Businessmen said that when conditions were good, there should be more money available. When conditions were bad, there should be less money in circulation. The Federal Reserve Act met this criticism. The Act allowed banks to issue money based upon the amount of business they were doing. The new law said that a bank note could be backed by commercial paper as well as by gold. Forty per cent of the backing was to be in gold and sixty per cent in paper. Commercial paper consists of notes that businessmen sign and give to banks when they borrow money. The notes say that the businessmen will repay the loans. Under the Federal Reserve Act, the more money a bank has lent to businessmen, the more dollars it can print and put into circulation. This system of issuing money is still in use.

The Federal Reserve Act also set up a Federal Reserve Banking System. Under this system, the nation was divided into twelve districts. A Federal Reserve Bank was established in each district to transact business with other banks. National banks had to become "members" of this system, and local banks could join it if they met certain requirements. Each member bank had to deposit a part of its funds with the Federal Reserve Bank in its district. When the member bank needed a lot of cash in a hurry, it did not have to call in its own loans. It could borrow money from the Federal Reserve

Bank. The law made it possible for banks to pool their reserves of money and help one another. Consequently, the banks became safer, and depositors were better protected.

Nearly all of the reforms that President Wilson wanted were passed during his first term in the White House. These reforms helped to put into practice the idea that government ought to protect the interests of all groups of people in the country. During Wilson's second term, however, the nation turned its attention to events abroad. In 1914 World War I began in Europe.

REVIEW ACTIVITIES

1. How did Theodore Roosevelt's policies differ from other Republican programs?
2. How did the secret ballot and the Seventeenth and Nineteenth Amendments help to make the government more democratic?
3. Point out some of the differences between President Wilson's *New Freedom* and President Roosevelt's *Square Deal.*
4. How does the Federal Reserve system differ from the system of National Banks?
5. During President Wilson's term, what new laws were passed to control business and help labor?

Select the words that best complete the following sentences. (*Please do not write in this book.*)

1. Theodore Roosevelt was called a _____ _____ because he enforced the Sherman _____ Act.
2. After 1906 the Interstate _____ Commission could decide what prices _____ could charge.
3. The right of voters to begin legislation is called _____.

When laws are referred directly to the voters, the process
is called _____.

4. Before 1900 United States senators were chosen by state
_____. Since 1913 senators have been elected by the
_____.

5. The Clayton Act helped unions. It made _____ and
_____ legal.

Who or what were the following:

1. Pure Food and Drug Act
2. Recall
3. Underwood Tariff Act
4. Sixteenth Amendment
5. Federal Trade Commission

CHAPTER **15**

America Grows Beyond Its Borders

THE UNITED STATES JOINED THE RACE FOR OVERSEAS POSSESSIONS

After the War of 1812 most Americans had little interest in foreign affairs. They were too busy at home pushing their boundaries across the continent toward the Pacific. Once the nation extended from coast to coast, there was still plenty to be done. The vast western frontier had to be settled, and industry had to be developed. So Americans set to work building railroads and factories and clearing land for new farms.

Meanwhile, in Europe, several countries were beginning to expand. Britain was the world's strongest naval power and had established colonies throughout the world. By the 1870's Germany and France began to compete with England for colonies and trade. All three nations set up colonies and trading stations in Africa and the Pacific. These outposts supplied valuable raw materials for home industries and new markets for manufacturers. They provided a place to invest money. They were useful, too, as naval bases where steamships could stop and take on a new supply of coal.

By forcing weaker countries to grant them colonies and trading rights, the European nations were following a policy known as *imperialism*. Americans do not like to think of the United States as imperialistic. The United States had bought Alaska from Russia in 1867, but this was mostly to keep Russia away from our borders. Then changes in American life led many people to have interests abroad.

During the second half of the nineteenth century, American industry started to produce more goods than it could sell at home. At the same time, the country began to need goods that could be bought only in foreign countries. So American businessmen asked the government for help. They wanted the government to get foreign markets for them. Now that they had enough money, they wanted a chance to invest it in foreign countries. And they wanted the government to protect their overseas investments. To do all these things the United States needed a strong navy.

Hawaii and Part of Samoa Became American Possessions

In 1890 the United States began to build up its naval strength. Ships were sent to protect Americans on the Samoan Islands in the Pacific Ocean. Before the century was over, the American government divided the Samoan Islands with Germany. The United States still holds the part of Samoa that it took over in 1899.

For some time American missionaries and sugar planters had been moving into the Hawaiian Islands. Then in 1891 the King of Hawaii died and his sister became queen. The new queen tried to keep white men from settling in the Islands. Americans on the Islands resented this and started a rebellion in 1893. The American government sent United States Marines to help them. They made the queen resign and asked that Hawaii be added to the United States. President Cleveland wanted the queen back in power, but she threatened to cut off the head of every man who had rebelled. So Cleveland decided to recognize Hawaii as an independent republic. In 1898 when the United States was at war with Spain, Hawaii became an American territory.

THE UNITED STATES WENT TO WAR WITH SPAIN

Although Americans were interested in the Pacific islands, they were more concerned about the countries of Latin America. These former Spanish colonies had never been able to keep stable governments. Thus it was always possible that some European power might try to take them over. The United States did not want this to happen. In 1823 President Monroe had warned Europe to leave the Western Hemisphere alone. This was still American policy. Consequently, when a dispute arose over the boundary between Venezuela and British Guiana, the United States demanded that the British settle the dispute peacefully. Secretary of State Richard Olney said, "The United States is practically sovereign on this continent." This was quite a claim, but the British were not willing to challenge it. They agreed to a compromise.

There were two main reasons for the American attitude toward Latin America. First, we felt that we had a right to run things in the western half of the world. This would help us to guard our national security. Second, we wished to protect the interests of American businessmen who had Latin American holdings. Both of these concerns made the United States interested in the Spanish colony of Cuba.

The Cuban Issue Excited Many Americans

In 1895 Cuba began a war for independence. Cubans bought guns in the United States and smuggled them into their country. The Spanish government sent troops to restore order. Many Cubans were put in concentration camps.

In the United States, newspapers began to print vivid stories of Spanish cruelty. Although some of these stories were true, many of them were greatly exaggerated. However, many Americans were willing to believe the stories, and a wave of anti-Spanish sentiment swept the country. People began to think that the United States should help set Cuba free. American businessmen with sugar plantations in Cuba were especially interested in overthrowing Spanish rule. They felt that their holdings there would be safer if Cuba were run by people more friendly to the United States.

In the meantime a new government had come to power in Spain. The leaders of this new government were anxious to avoid war with the United States. They started several reforms in Cuba and promised to give the Cuban people a chance to govern themselves. But these reforms came too late. On the night of February 15, 1898, the American battleship *Maine* was blown up while riding at anchor in Havana harbor. To this day no one knows who was responsible for the tragedy. But many Americans were willing to blame it on the Spanish government. People throughout the country began to clamor for war.

After the *Maine* was sunk the United States demanded that Spain end the fighting and set free all of the Cubans that they had put in concentration camps. The Spanish government agreed but asked for time. President McKinley was willing to give them the time, but Congress was not. Finally McKinley gave in to the public feeling. On April 25, 1898, the United States declared war on Spain.

A Short War Helped to Make the United States a World Power

The first action in the Spanish-American War took place not in Cuba but in the Philippine Islands. These islands belonged to Spain. An American naval squadron under Commodore George Dewey sailed into Manila Bay and forced the Spaniards to surrender. A short time later, American troops arrived to occupy the Philippines.

In June troops landed in Cuba and fought their way toward Santiago. On July 3 the American fleet defeated the Spanish fleet in Santiago harbor. Then the Spanish troops in Cuba surrendered. Meanwhile, American troops had occupied the nearby island of Puerto Rico. With her army and navy defeated, Spain asked for peace. The fighting had lasted about 115 days.

At the peace conference, Spain agreed to give Cuba its independence. She gave Puerto Rico to the United States along with the Pacific island of Guam. She also gave us the Philippines in return for a payment of 20 million dollars. Meanwhile, Congress had made Hawaii an American territory. Thus, during the year 1898, the United States became a world power with distant colonies to defend. We could no longer think only of our own homeland.

NEW POSSESSIONS BROUGHT NEW RESPONSIBILITIES

There were many Americans who still felt that the United States should not have colonies. The question became a big issue in the presidential election of 1900. By this time the people in the Philippines had started to rebel against United States rule. The Democrats and their candidate, William Jennings Bryan, demanded that the United States give up its colonies. But the Republicans, led by William McKinley, took pride in America's expansion. They talked about opportunities for trade and about making the colonies civilized. They talked about America's place in the world. The Republicans won the election.

It took the United States almost three years to put down the Philippine rebellion. Military rule was ended in 1901. The next year the people of the Philippine Islands were allowed to elect part of their legislature. The United States tried to make the Philippines democratic. Gradually the people were given a bigger share in their government. But the United States kept the Philippines as a colony. They were granted their complete independence shortly after the end of World War II.

In Cuba the Spanish-American War put an end to Spanish rule. Cuba was independent. But American troops remained on the island for two years. When the Cubans drew up a constitution, the United States made them add the following provisions: 1) Cuba must never give any foreign power control over the island; 2) Cuba must not go too far into debt; 3) the United States could step in at any time to keep order or to protect Cuba from other powers; and 4) the United States could buy or rent land for naval bases. These conditions made Cuba only partly free. The Cubans did not like them, but they had to agree.

In the years that followed, the Cuban government borrowed money from New York bankers. Whenever these bankers thought the Cuban government could not pay back what it owed, they threatened to have American soldiers take over Cuba's tax collection. American businessmen bought thousands of acres of Cuban sugar land. They built plants to refine the sugar. The threat of United States troops kept Cuban factory workers and farm laborers from striking. These conditions enabled American bankers and businessmen to make money. They did not make the Cubans like the United States.

AMERICA BUILT THE PANAMA CANAL

Ever since the California Gold Rush of 1849, Americans had been interested in building a canal across Central America to link the Atlantic and Pacific Oceans. Such a canal would greatly shorten the length of sea voyages between our eastern and western coasts. By using the canal, ships could make this trip without going all the way around South America.

Back in 1850 the United States had agreed with Great Britain that neither country would build a canal alone. At that time Great Britain was strong and the United States was weak; so it seemed to be a good arrangement for America. Then in 1878 a French company started to build a canal across the narrow Isthmus of Panama. Disease killed many workers and the company failed. By 1900 the Americans were ready to build the canal. The first step was to get Great Britain to cancel the treaty of 1850. In 1901 Great Britain agreed to let the United States build the canal alone, but insisted that charges for using the canal should be the same for all nations. So the United States bought the French company's rights in Panama, which belonged to the South American nation of Colombia. However, Colombia would not permit the work to begin. The Colombian government wanted more money than the United States was willing to pay. Fearing that the canal might be built somewhere else, a group of leaders in Panama started a revolt against Colombia. When Colombian troops were sent to put down the revolt, United States warships would not let them enter Panama. The revolution succeeded and the new government of Panama gave the United States the right to build a canal. Panama also gave the United States a ten-mile wide strip of land across Panama. This land is called the Canal Zone. For the use of the Canal Zone, the United States pays $250,000 rent to the Republic of Panama every year.

The building of the Panama Canal took ten years and cost about 380 million dollars. The first ship passed through the canal in 1914. By taking over the Canal Zone, the United States added to its power in the Caribbean Sea. But we did not win any friends in Colombia.

THE UNITED STATES SENT TROOPS INTO OTHER COUNTRIES

The United States gained the right to build the Panama Canal during the administration of President Theodore Roosevelt. Roosevelt's dealings with Colombia were typical of his dealings with other Latin American nations. He believed in using the threat of United States force to get these nations to do what he wanted.

Roosevelt Added a Corollary to the Monroe Doctrine

Several Latin American nations were in debt to European bankers. Sometimes they either could not or would not pay their debts. So Roosevelt decided to act as a "policeman" for this half of the world. He told the Latin Americans that they had nothing to fear as long as they paid the money they owed. However, should they fail to do so, the United States would have to step in and take over their financial affairs. Otherwise, said Roosevelt, the European nations would have an excuse to interfere in Latin America. This policy was known as the Roosevelt Corollary to the Monroe Doctrine.

Roosevelt had a chance to put his new policy to use. The little Dominican Republic, located on an island in the Caribbean, owed European bankers more than 30 million dollars. Secretary of State John Hay put pressure on the Dominican Republic's government. Hay got the Dominicans to let the United States take charge of their financial matters. American officials moved into the country and collected taxes. Part of this money went to the Dominican government. The rest was used to pay off the European bankers.

After Roosevelt left office, the United States continued with the same kind of policy. In 1911 the government of Nicaragua needed money. American bankers lent Nicaragua the needed funds. But the United States made Nicaragua agree to have an American collect all of the import taxes in that country. A year later, a revolt threatened Nicaragua.

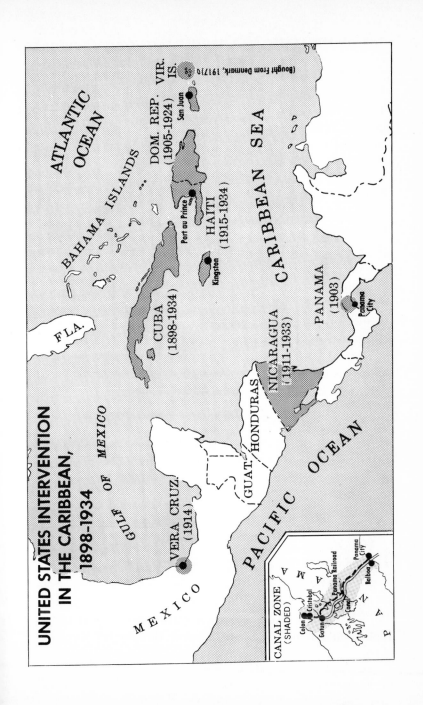

UNITED STATES INTERVENTION IN THE CARIBBEAN, 1898-1934

ATLANTIC OCEAN

BAHAMA ISLANDS

VIR. IS.

Bought from Denmark, 1917)

DOM. REP. (1905-1924)

San Juan

HAITI (1915-1934)

Port au Prince

Kingston

CUBA (1898-1934)

CARIBBEAN SEA

FLA.

GULF OF MEXICO

PANAMA (1903)

Panama City

NICARAGUA (1911-1933)

HONDURAS

GUAT.

PACIFIC OCEAN

VERA CRUZ. (1914)

MEXICO

CANAL ZONE (SHADED)

Colon

Cristobal

Gatun

Panama Railroad

Canal

Panama City

Balboa

PANAMA

To make sure that the loans were paid back, the United States sent Marines into Nicaragua to keep order.

WILSON TRIED DIPLOMATIC PRESSURE INSTEAD OF FORCE

Many Americans did not approve of sending soldiers abroad to help collect loans for American bankers. One such American was Woodrow Wilson, who won the presidential election in 1912.

For years Americans had invested money in Mexico. They got rights to open up mines, drill for oil, and build railroads. Profits from these ventures went to the United States. Most Mexicans remained poor. Beginning in 1910 there was a series of revolts in Mexico. The revolutionists wanted the wealth of Mexico to remain in Mexico. The Mexican revolutionists wanted to take away the property of Americans.

President Wilson had to protect American rights. But he did not want to send troops into Mexico. He tried to put pressure on Mexico in a different way. After the President of Mexico was murdered in 1913, Wilson refused to recognize the new government in Mexico. He said that the United States would not deal with men who came into power by murder. Wilson's attitude was new. Before this time the United States recognized any government that was actually in power. Wilson used his position as President to make things difficult for a foreign government that he disliked. The United States still follows today Wilson's policy of "nonrecognition." For example, our government does not recognize the Communist governments of Cuba and Red China.

Wilson Sent Troops to Mexico and Haiti

Diplomatic pressure did not solve all of our problems with our southern neighbors. Wilson found that he had to use the army after all. The new President of Mexico was not able to keep order. A bandit leader named Pancho Villa set himself up in northern Mexico. On two different occasions, Villa led raids into United States territory. When the Mexican government could not control him, the United States sent an army under General John J. Pershing onto Mexican soil.

Wilson also sent soldiers to the Republic of Haiti. A series of revolutions between 1911 and 1915 had left that country in disorder. American businessmen in Haiti demanded protection. An American force landed on the island in 1915.

Soldiers seized the customs houses, and the American commander threatened to occupy Haiti with American troops. In this way the United States made Haiti adopt a new constitution that gave American citizens special rights. An American would supervise taxation and money matters. United States Army officers would supervise the Haitian police. Haiti became a country occupied by United States military forces. Over 1,500 people were killed when American Marines put down revolts. The Americans built new roads in Haiti, opened schools, and established order. But the people of Haiti preferred freedom. Most Haitians came to hate American rule.

Revolts also occurred in the Dominican Republic. In 1914 the United States sent a warship there. An election was held under the supervision of the United States Marines. There was another revolution in 1916. Then the United States Navy simply took over the Dominican Republic. American soldiers stayed there until 1924. American businessmen ran the Dominican Republic's treasury until 1941.

By interfering in Latin American affairs, the United States made many enemies among her neighbors. Latin Americans did not want to be told how to run their countries. But American leaders felt that the United States had to protect its own interests in the best way it could. As a result, it was some time before we changed our policies in an effort to win Latin American friendship. Before this happened, the world was plunged into a great war.

REVIEW ACTIVITIES

1. Why did the United States enter the race for overseas possessions?
2. Why did the United States go to war against Spain?
3. What special provisions was the United States given in Cuba after the war?
4. Roosevelt added a corollary to the Monroe Doctrine. What was it? Where and how was it used?
5. Many Latin Americans dislike the United States. Can you explain why?

Select the words that best complete the following sentences. (*Please do not write in this book.*)

1. As a result of the _____ War, Cuba gained its _____.

2. After the Spanish-American War, Spain gave Puerto Rico to the United States along with the Pacific island of _____. We also obtained the _____ in return for a payment of 20 million dollars.

3. The Republic of Panama leases the _____ _____ to the United States for a yearly rental of _____.

4. In an effort to protect American rights in Mexico, President _____ tried to put pressure on the _____ _____ by refusing to recognize it.

5. This policy of "non-recognition" is still in use today, and the United States does not deal officially with the Communist governments of _____ and _____ _____.

Who or what were the following:

1. Imperialism
2. Samoan Islands
3. The *Maine*
4. The Hawaiian Islands
5. Haiti

CHAPTER **16**

World War I

WORLD WAR I BEGAN IN EUROPE

In 1914 a war broke out among the biggest powers in Europe. This was the first large European war since the time of the French Revolution. In those days Washington, Adams and Jefferson had tried to keep the country out of war. The United States wanted no "entangling alliances." In the end, though, the United States had become involved. The United States entered the War of 1812 in order to protect American ships and to make our western borders secure.

One hundred years later, in 1914, almost the same thing happened. The United States was concerned with its own affairs. At home people were trying to bring about needed reforms. In Latin America we were protecting the interests of the United States. Europe was not our concern. Just the same, America entered the war about three years after it had begun.

Europe Was Divided into Two Armed Camps

For some time European countries had been divided into two alliances. England, France and Russia were allied on one side. Germany, Austria and Italy were on the other side. Businessmen in these European countries were rivals. Their industries needed new markets and new raw materials. Each country tried to get colonies in order to improve its trade. To protect their home markets, countries put up tariffs against one another. They built larger armies and navies.

In this rivalry, Germany got a later start than France and England. Consequently, England and France had the best colonies. Germany had to take whatever was left. Whenever Germany tried to get special trade advantages, England objected. If Germany built a new battleship, England built two. The German Emperor said all that Germany wanted was "a place in the sun." Germans thought that the English and the French were holding them back. They built their army bigger and bigger. Europe was divided into two armed camps. Only a small incident was needed to involve the two alliances in a full-scale war.

An Assassination Touched Off the War

This incident was supplied in 1914 in Bosnia, a province of Austria. A Serbian patriot murdered the Austrian Archduke, Francis Ferdinand. Austria threatened to invade Serbia. Russia wanted to help Serbia and got her army ready to fight. Germany seemed to think that Russia was going to attack Austria. So Germany attacked first, but she moved against Russia's ally, France.

In August of 1914 Germany attacked France. German armies marched into France through Belgium—although Belgium was supposed to be neutral. England and Russia had promised by treaty to join France. Italy and Austria had promised to join Germany. Austria went to war, but Italy did not. Later the Italians came into the war on the side of the French.

Germany hoped for a short war, but the first attacks were not completely successful. The war settled down to a new kind of fighting. Soldiers dug trenches all across the northern part of France.

AMERICA TRIED TO REMAIN NEUTRAL

In America, President Wilson hoped the United States could keep out of the war. He said America would be neutral. As the war dragged on, most Americans began to feel that France and England stood for what was right and that they ought to win. There were several reasons for this. First of all, Germany had attacked first. It looked as though Germany was trying to use military power to force her will on Europe. Second, Germany had broken her promise to keep Belgium neutral. Third, both England and France had democratic governments like our own. Germany, on the other hand, was more military and less democratic. In addition, German submarines began to sink ordinary merchant ships on the high seas. Germany's best weapon on the ocean was the submarine. But a submarine cannot save the lives of seamen and passengers on a sinking ship. This was a new kind of warfare. Americans thought it was both illegal and cruel. Germans said they had to use submarines because of what England's navy was doing.

England's navy was large and strong. It drove the German navy from the oceans all over the world. The British navy also prevented Americans from trading with Germany. According to international law this was illegal, and the American government protested. But England went right on stopping American ships from going to Germany. However, American manufacturers and American shipowners did not lose money. There was plenty of demand for American goods in England and France. Therefore the United States did not protest too strongly.

Germany wanted to stop American goods from going to England. Since her navy was not very strong, Germany had to use submarines.

In 1915 Germany warned Americans that her submarines would sink any English or French merchant ship, even if Americans or American goods were on board. This time President Wilson protested to Germany. But the Germans still sank merchant ships anyway. On May 7, 1915, a German submarine sank the *Lusitania,* a British passenger ship. Of the 1,198 persons drowned, 128 were Americans.

Wilson Tried to Protect American Shipping

Some people in the United States thought that Americans should not travel on ships owned by any of the fighting nations. Others, including President Wilson, wanted to defend the right of Americans to travel as they pleased. In this, Wilson was doing what Presidents Jefferson and Madison had done before the War of 1812.

When elections were held in the United States in 1916, President Wilson was popular. He had put many reforms through Congress and he had kept America out of the war. The Republicans opposed Wilson's reforms. They were ready to help Great Britain in the war. They felt that Great Britain was fighting for the right cause. The Republican Party nominated Charles Evans Hughes as their candidate. Wilson won the election with the slogan, "He kept us out of war."

Then conditions changed. Germany was not winning the war. The British and French had one advantage. They could import goods from America. So the Germans announced that they would sink any ship heading for England or France, even if it belonged to the United States. President Wilson tried to get the Germans not to sink merchant and passenger ships, but he failed.

To protect our vessels, President Wilson used an old law that gave him power to put guns on merchant ships. Still the Germans sank three American ships in March of 1917 alone. By this time American feeling against Germany was strong. In April President Wilson asked Congress to declare war. The United States wanted no territory, he said, and no colonies. The United States wanted to fight only for "the rights of nations, great and small." "The world," said Wilson, "must be made safe for democracy." By April 6 the United States was officially in the war.

New Agencies Helped Organize the War Effort

To help win the war, the United States had to use all its strength. The American navy immediately joined the fight against German submarines. But the American army was small, and it took time to build it up. Meanwhile, America's part in the war was to provide goods and supplies.

Congress set up a War Industries Board to speed production of war materials. The Board also cut down on the manufacture of unnecessary goods. Then the government took over all of the railroads in the United States and combined them into a single railway system. This made it possible to ship war materials more quickly. The United States Shipping Board began to operate American merchant ships. More ships were built to carry men and supplies to the war zone in Europe. President Wilson appointed a food administrator to increase farm production and cut down on the amount of food that civilians ate. A fuel administrator helped to increase the production of coal. People had to use less coal so that industries would have all the power they needed. Congress also set up a National War Labor Board. Everybody agreed that the nation could not afford strikes. The War Labor Board helped to settle disputes about wages and hours.

When America entered the war, very few soldiers were ready to fight. In May of 1917 Congress passed the Selective Service Act or "draft." According to this law, all male citizens in the United States between the ages of 21 and 30 could be drafted. The Army built camps where new soldiers could be trained.

The first small group of American soldiers reached France in June, 1917, commanded by General John J. Pershing. By the end of 1917, there were already five American divisions in France. Each division had 28,000 men.

Germany Was Defeated

By March of 1918, German generals saw that their submarine campaign was failing. American troops and supplies were reaching France in a steady stream. German armies made a final effort to capture Paris. To meet the attack, American troops filled up holes in the British and French lines. They fought along the Marne River at Chateau-Thierry and Belleau Wood. In late summer a separate American army took charge of the eastern end of the long battle line. This army drove the Germans out of St. Mihiel.

Late in September the allies began to attack. American soldiers drove forward into the Argonne Forest. Everywhere the Germans were forced back. Early in November the German Emperor resigned and fled to the Netherlands. On November 11 an armistice was signed and the war was over.

WILSON HOPED TO BUILD A LASTING PEACE

In the words of President Wilson, Americans had fought "to make the world safe for democracy." Wilson thought the peace treaty should provide for democratic governments everywhere. He also thought that it should arrange world affairs so as to make another world war impossible. In January of 1918 Wilson had stated what he wanted the peace treaty to include. In an address to Congress, he outlined his famous *Fourteen Points* for a lasting peace. Some of the most important things the President wanted were: 1) In place of the Empires of Germany and Austria, there should be democratic countries each made up of people all speaking the same language. 2) Colonies in Asia and Africa should have more democratic governments. 3) All nations should give up big armies and navies and make no more secret treaties of alliance. 4) Nations should lower their tariffs and remove other bars to trade. 5) Ships of neutral nations should be free to trade in war time. 6) Finally, all countries should join in a League of Nations where disputes between them could be settled in peace.

Wilson's Fourteen Points created quite a stir among the people of Europe. They won the American President a great deal of friendship and prestige. When the war ended, many Europeans expected these points to form the basis of the peace treaty. The Germans, in particular, hoped that this would be the case. Wilson's plan seemed too dream-like to the leaders of France and England. They wanted mostly to be sure that Germany could do no more fighting. When the Armistice was signed, they made Germany give up all big guns, all airplanes, all submarines. Germany also had to hand over most of her navy and many railroad trains. Allied troops then occupied all of Germany west of the Rhine.

England and France Would Not Accept the Fourteen Points

The formal peace conference began early in 1919 in Versailles, France. President Wilson went in person. Thirty-two governments sent delegates, but most decisions were made by four men: Wilson; David Lloyd-George, the British Prime Minister; Georges Clemenceau, the leader of France; and Vittorio Orlando of Italy. Germany had no part in making the treaty.

As the talks progressed, it became quite apparent that

Clemenceau and Lloyd-George did not want to accept Wilson's idea of "peace without victory." Clemenceau was an aging man who had been active in the French government for a long while. He could remember a time nearly fifty years before when Germany had defeated France and the French had been forced to accept harsh terms. He wanted to adjust the boundaries between France and Germany to give France a better chance to defend herself against future German attacks. He also wanted France to acquire the valuable iron and coal producing territories that had helped to build Germany's war machine. He wanted revenge.

Lloyd-George of England wanted to reduce Germany's ability to compete with England in world trade. He wanted England to acquire some of Germany's overseas possessions.

In the face of this opposition, Wilson gradually weakened his stand. He made several concessions on his Fourteen Points so that the other delegates would adopt his favorite project, the League of Nations.

THE TREATY OF VERSAILLES PUNISHED GERMANY

When the Treaty of Versailles was completed, it was presented to the German representatives. Its terms were fairly harsh. Germany had to surrender territory to France and the new republic of Poland. She had to give up all of her colonies. Her army was limited to 100,000 men, and her navy was reduced to six battleships and no submarines. Germany was to pay large amounts of money to the victorious allies for war damages and costs. These were called *reparations,* and the total bill was nearly 32 billion dollars. Germany had to sign the treaty.

The peace conference made other adjustments on the map of Europe. The Austrian Empire was broken up. A new nation called Czechoslovakia was created. Serbia was enlarged and renamed Yugoslavia. Although Wilson was not happy with the Treaty of Versailles as a whole, he was proud of one part. This was the provision for a League of Nations.

The League of Nations was to provide a way for nations to work together. It was to have a permanent office staff. There would be an assembly made up of delegates from all member nations. And there would be a council made up of nine members. The United States would always be a member of this council. The League of Nations also included a plan for making colonial powers responsible to the League. Countries that took over former German colonies would have to make reports to the League of Nations.

America Refused to Join the League of Nations

In brief, this was the treaty that President Wilson asked the American people to accept. Even before the treaty was finished, many American leaders objected to the League of Nations. Some of them believed that the United States should not join in such a League. They thought that America should let the rest of the world settle its own problems.

In the election of 1918, a few days before the armistice was signed, the Republicans had won a majority in both houses of Congress. The Republicans campaigned against Wilson's treaty. They said that the United States should not be involved in a League of Nations. It was too idealistic. Many people tended to agree with them. Americans had bought savings bonds, saved on food and made sacrifices. They had joined a crusade to make the world safe for democracy. Now Americans were tired of hard work and sacrifices. They were tired of high ideals and foreign wars. They wanted to return to the good old days.

This was the spirit Wilson had to fight to get his treaty accepted. He knew that Republicans were opposing him, but he thought that enough people would give him support. In spite of Republican attacks on the Treaty of Versailles, a majority of senators favored it. In the beginning, most people were probably in favor of it too. But a treaty has to be accepted by two-thirds of the Senate, and the Republicans controlled enough votes to stop its passage. The Senate talked for weeks while American idealism died down. Republicans hoped that enthusiasm for Wilson's cause would cool off.

Although he was ill, Wilson went on a speaking trip to defend the League of Nations. He spoke in cities and towns all across the country. But one day in Pueblo, Colorado, he suffered a stroke from which he never really recovered.

Wilson lost his battle for the League of Nations. He had tried to make Americans see that the United States was now too big to live alone in the world. He had tried to make America a leader in world affairs. He wanted the United States to help the League of Nations keep the world at peace.

Apparently the country was not ready for his vision. In November of 1919 the Senate rejected the League of Nations. In the election of 1920 the Democratic Party stood for the League, and they lost. The Republican Party was lukewarm or against the League, and the Republicans won. Their candidate was Warren G. Harding of Ohio.

As soon as Harding became President, Congress declared the war at an end. The United States signed its own peace treaties with Austria and Germany. Other countries set up the League of Nations for which America's Woodrow Wilson had fought so hard. The United States stayed out of it. Americans settled down to enjoy "normalcy," as Harding put it.

AMERICANS BECAME FEARFUL OF FOREIGNERS

It was hard for Americans to know what was normal. They had wanted to live alone and to concern themselves only with America. They had wanted the rest of the world to take care of its own problems. Yet they had become involved with foreigners in a foreign war. Many Americans began to think that taking part in the war had been a mistake. They felt that we had been tricked into it by other countries. They became fearful of foreigners in general and their fear turned to anger. The Ku Klux Klan was revived. Its members tried to frighten foreigners in the United States.

Many Americans were afraid of the foreign idea called communism. Communists were against our capitalistic economic system, and they wished to overthrow our democratic government. They preached a world revolution of workers. The only Communistic country in the world was Russia.

During the war there had been a revolution in Russia. Nicholas II, the last of a long line of Russian czars, was overthrown. So was the democratic government that followed him. The Communists took charge of Russia in 1917. They withdrew their country from the war against Germany. They tried to start Communist revolutions in other countries. Several democratic countries—including the United States—sent soldiers to Russia to try to dislodge the Communist government. But the Communists stayed in power.

Strikes and Violence Added to American Fears

A few American labor leaders were Communists. Some Americans thought labor unions were Communistic, too. When labor unions wanted to keep the high wages and advantages they had won during the war, employers objected. They said the unions were Communistic.

In 1919 a wave of strikes swept the country. Steel workers demanded an eight-hour day. They wanted unions in all the steel mills. Even the Boston police went on strike. There were several bomb explosions, the worst one occurring on Wall Street in New York City. People became alarmed. It seemed as though foreigners and Communists were trying to blow up the country. People feared that the country was in danger of a Communist revolution.

Under Attorney General Palmer, federal agents made thousands of arrests. The United States deported 500 aliens.

Hundreds more were kept in federal prisons. The Legislature of New York expelled five members because they were Socialists, even though they had been properly elected to the legislature. Two foreigners in Massachusetts named Sacco and Vanzetti were arrested for murder. The evidence against them was slight, but they were found guilty and condemned to death. Many people thought that they were condemned only because they were foreigners.

Immigration Was Restricted

Suspicion of foreigners led to a demand for new legislation to change our immigration policies. By 1921 nearly 800,000 foreign-born immigrants were entering the United States every year. In 1924 Congress passed an act that limited immigration. After 1927 only 150,000 immigrants were allowed into this country each year. The law also said that no one would be admitted unless he could become a citizen. Since an earlier law had said that Orientals could not become citizens, the new act had the effect of excluding all people from China and Japan. The Japanese, in particular, resented this legislation.

The Tariff Remained High

Americans could try to keep "America for Americans." They could stay out of the League of Nations. But the United States continued to become involved in foreign affairs. For one thing, Americans found that they could not collect the money that their allies had borrowed during the war. The United States had lent more than 10 billion dollars to the allied nations of Europe. It was difficult now for these nations to pay back the loans. They wanted to sell their goods in the United States. But Congress passed a high tariff law in 1922, and this kept their goods out. Congressional leaders refused to make any changes. They demanded payment. For a while, most countries that owed money to the United States managed to pay some of it back. However, in 1929 there was a world-wide depression. After that the payments stopped altogether.

THE UNITED STATES SIGNED AGREEMENTS TO AVOID ANOTHER WAR

Meanwhile, the United States found itself in an arms race. After the war, Japan began to build up a big navy. To keep ahead of Japan, the United States also began to build warships. Soon England entered the race in order to keep her navy as large as ours. It seemed that the same type of rivalry that had helped to bring about World War I was starting all over again. Finally, the United States decided to act. In 1921 Secretary of State Charles Evans Hughes called a conference in Washington. Hughes proposed that governments limit the size of their navies. He suggested that they build no new battleships for ten years. As a result, five nations at the Washington conference signed a treaty. The treaty provided that for every five ships that America and Great Britain had, Japan could have three. A conference in London, held during 1930, continued this agreement for five more years.

In 1928 the United States entered another agreement to keep the peace. This agreement was named after Secretary of State Frank Kellog and Aristide Briand, the foreign minister of France. A total of fifteen nations signed the Kellog-Briand Pact in Paris. Later, nearly every other government signed it. The nations involved simply agreed to "renounce war as an instrument of national policy." This was a noble idea, but there was no way to enforce it.

The United States had helped to win a war for democracy, but it refused to do anything for democracy afterward. America stayed out of the League of Nations. America imposed high tariffs and still tried to collect war debts from other democracies. The United States did lead in planning for a holiday in the building of battleships. And an American Secretary of State had drawn up an idealistic pact to outlaw war. But all this did not add up to leadership. The world expected more. The world needed more from the richest democratic nation on earth. It took another world war to convince Americans that a powerful nation, even a powerful democracy, cannot live alone in the world.

Meanwhile, democracy in the United States was tested by a tragic depression.

REVIEW ACTIVITIES

1. What conditions in the early 1900's divided the nations of Europe into two armed camps? How were these nations divided?
2. Why did most Americans side with England and France?
3. What were some of the new agencies set up in the United States to help organize the war effort?
4. President Wilson announced his Fourteen Points, or suggestions for a peace treaty. What were some of his proposals? Why were they opposed by the Senate?
5. What problems did the United States face after World War I? What steps were taken to solve these problems?

Select the words that best complete the following sentences. (*Please do not write in this book.*)

1. When the United States entered World War I, President Wilson said it was to protect the rights of _____ and make the world safe for _____.
2. According to the _____ _____ Act, passed in 1917, all male citizens in the United States between the ages of 21 and 30 could be _____.
3. The treaty that ended World War I was called the Treaty of _____. It set up a League of _____ to provide

a way for countries to work together to keep world peace.

4. During World War I there was a _____ in Russia. The Czar was overthrown and _____ took charge of the country in 1917.

5. The _____ Pact was signed in Paris in 1928. It was an agreement to _____ war.

Who or what were the following:

1. Archduke Francis Ferdinand
2. The *Lusitania*
3. Reparations
4. Sacco and Vanzetti
5. Immigration Act of 1924

CHAPTER 17

Prosperity and Depression

AMERICA ENTERED THE MAD DECADE

After World War I, Americans had ten years of prosperity —from 1919 to 1929. Then came a depression and ten years of poor business, unemployment and "the New Deal."

Good times did not come immediately after the war. There were difficult times at first. Factories that made tanks and guns during the war had to change over and make automobiles and machines. Returning soldiers had to find employment. Wartime workers in shipyards had to find new jobs. When the workers and unions tried to keep the high wages they had received in wartime, there were strikes. But by 1921, when Warren Harding became President, the biggest problems seemed to be over.

Although prosperity returned, "normalcy" did not. There were changes in the way that people acted. These were so startling that the 1920's are called the "mad decade."

After the war, many people seemed to want to "live it up." They were disappointed because the war did not solve all of the world's problems. They could not see that the suffering and killing during the war had done any good. They forgot the high ideals of wartime.

There were scandals in the government. Early in the 1920's the head of the Veterans Bureau was sent to prison for fraud. The man in charge of all the German property that America took over during the war also was imprisoned. The most famous plot of all was the Teapot Dome scandal that involved Secretary of the Interior Albert B. Fall. Fall accepted money from friends to let them rent United States oil lands. He was fined and sent to prison.

Prohibition Was Difficult to Enforce

Dishonesty was not confined to government circles. Other people also disobeyed laws—especially the law that made it illegal to make or sell alcoholic drinks. For years many people had thought that drinking was an evil that should be prohibited by law. During the war Congress had proposed the Eighteenth Amendment to the Constitution. This Amendment would give Congress power to prohibit the making or selling of alcoholic drinks. It was ratified by the states and went into effect in 1919. Congress then passed the Volstead Act to enforce the Eighteenth Amendment.

Most people obeyed the law, but many did not. They were willing to buy liquor in defiance of the law. Men who supplied the liquor were called "bootleggers." Many gangsters became bootleggers and earned enormous profits. They often bribed policemen and other government officials. They hired gunmen to protect them, and sometimes their gunmen killed rival bootleggers. The most famous bootlegger of all was Al Capone of Chicago. Illegal places in which alcoholic beverages were served began to spring up. They were called "speakeasies." People who otherwise obeyed the law went to these speakeasies. Some even made their own liquor at home. Prohibition was so hard to enforce and so widely disobeyed that it was finally repealed in 1933.

The Country Underwent Many Changes

The post-war years also saw a change in the place of women. Some women had demanded the right to vote even before the Civil War. As time went on, more women went to school, took jobs in business and received equal property rights. In 1920 the Nineteenth Amendment was added to the Constitution. This gave women the right to vote.

Women showed their independence in other ways as well. They bobbed their hair and smoked in public. They wore short skirts. They even went to speakeasies.

Forms of art changed too. "Modern" painting and serious "modern" music appeared. Popular music like jazz and popular dances like the Charleston, seemed far from normal to many people. All these—scandals, freedom for women, jazz and speakeasies—were signs of restlessness. But the country was prosperous and business was better than ever.

THE 1920's WERE PROSPEROUS YEARS

For the Republican Party which came to power in 1921, "normalcy" meant that business would be free from government interference. It also meant high tariffs.

In 1922 Congress passed the Fordney-McCumber Tariff Act. This Act raised tariff duties even higher than they had been under President Taft. Republicans said that the new tariff would help business. Many businessmen disagreed. American business, they said, no longer needed protection.

Europe Found It Hard to Trade with the United States

Until 1918 America as a whole owed money abroad. Many immigrants had borrowed money in Europe to pay for their passage to America. Americans had borrowed money from European bankers to buy land, build railroads and set up factories. They paid interest on the money, and they paid back their loans in dollars. Europeans used these dollars to buy American products. During the war, Europeans used up all their American money to buy food and war supplies. Afterwards, Europeans owed Americans money. Now they had far fewer dollars to pay for American grain or American factory-made goods. This meant that American businessmen had a hard time selling their goods abroad. Some Americans argued that we should lower our tariffs and let Europeans sell their goods here. This would help the Europeans to buy American goods, and this might improve our position in the world market. But Congress would not lower the tariff.

The effects of America's trade policy did not show up for years. American factories continued to make money. People who had not bought things during the war began to spend their savings. They bought the food, clothing and houses that they could not buy in wartime. In addition, there were new products which they could buy, like refrigerators, vacuum cleaners and radios.

Harding and Coolidge Let Business Alone

The country went on a building spree. States and counties built bridges and concrete highways. Businessmen built service stations, restaurants, tourist homes and office buildings. Fortunes were made in the movie industry. Factories made profits. Prices on the stock market went up. Nearly everybody seemed to be sharing in the country's general prosperity.

President Harding and the Republican Party took credit for this prosperity. They said that the United States was prosperous because they were keeping a high tariff and leaving business alone. They continued these policies. During the 1920's big business was as free to operate as it had ever been.

Before President Harding had been in office for two years,

he died. Then Vice-President Calvin Coolidge stepped into the White House. Coolidge also let business leaders alone. The country prospered and taxes were reduced. The government began to pay off the national debt.

THE NATION'S ECONOMY WAS UNSTABLE

Satisfied with Coolidge's performance, the Republicans nominated him to run for the presidency in 1924. The Democrats nominated John W. Davis of West Virginia. Coolidge won the election and the Republicans won control of Congress. While Coolidge was President, the country remained prosperous. It seemed that the Republicans were right; their policies did bring good times to everyone. But American prosperity was built on sand. Three things were wrong.

First of all, American farmers did not share in the prosperity. During the war they were paid high prices for grain and livestock because so much of it was needed to feed the armed forces. Farmers put more land to the plow. They borrowed money to buy new machinery. When the war was over, they could produce more wheat, cotton and meat than they could sell. Foreign countries that had bought American wheat now were unable to get the money to pay for American produce. Farm prices went way down and many farmers went bankrupt. Banks that had lent money to farmers also failed. Farmers asked the federal government for help.

In 1923 Congress passed an Agricultural Credits Act. This Act enabled farmers to borrow money at low rates of interest, but it did not raise the price of grain and meat. The real problem was that farmers were producing too much. In 1924 Congress planned to set up a federal board with the power to buy up extra farm produce. This "surplus" produce could be sold abroad. However, President Coolidge vetoed the act. He said that it would raise prices at home. Farmers wondered why it was all right for businessmen to charge high prices and not all right for farmers to be allowed to do the same thing.

In 1929 Congress passed the Agricultural Marketing Act that set up a Federal Farm Board with power to buy surplus grain and store it until the price went up. The government kept buying grain and storing it for some time, but the price never went up. Finally, the Farm Board had to stop buying produce altogether. Over-expansion kept farm prices low.

Second, business expanded very rapidly during the 1920's. But there was a limit to the amount of goods that the American people could buy. Before the 1920's most people paid cash for the goods they bought. When ready cash became scarce, dealers began to sell goods on time. They arranged for buyers to pay in monthly installments. But factory owners did not know how many cars, refrigerators and radios people would be able to buy. To businessmen it seemed that people would go on buying the products of American factories forever. Factories borrowed money and built new plants. By 1928 products were harder to sell. Buyers had less money.

Third, prices on the stock market rose too high. People with little business experience began to buy stocks. But these people did not study the situation. They thought that the factories would continue to make money. They expected the prices of stock to keep going higher and higher. These people were too optimistic. Many companies produced more than they could sell. A few men who were aware of business conditions realized that stocks were priced too high. Banks that had lent money for people to buy stock began to worry. But Americans kept on buying stock anyway. A few experts said that there would be a slump. President Coolidge, on the other hand, said that the American business system was sound.

THE GREAT DEPRESSION BEGAN IN 1929

In 1928 Coolidge "did not choose to run for President." The Republican Party nominated Herbert Hoover, Coolidge's

Secretary of Commerce. Hoover had been an engineer. Born poor, he had become a millionaire.

The Democrats nominated Governor Alfred Smith of New York. Smith was opposed to prohibition. He felt that the Eighteenth Amendment should be repealed. Many people who thought that drinking was an evil would not vote for Smith. Others would not vote for him because he was a Roman Catholic.

As a result, Hoover won the election. Almost immediately Congress passed a new tariff law. The Hawley-Smoot Act raised tariffs higher than ever. This time high tariffs did not make the country prosper. Within six months after President Hoover took office, the stock market collapsed.

During the summer of 1929, wise investors began to withdraw their money from the stock market. Late in October of the same year, everybody tried to sell his stock. Prices went down so fast that the people who had borrowed money to buy stocks could not sell them soon enough. Many of them were never able to pay back what they owed. The brokers and bankers who had lent them the money suffered too.

The stock market crash in October of 1929 was only the first in a series of business failures. People quickly lost their optimism about the future. They stopped buying things that they could not afford. Factories had to lay off workers, and some of them shut down. Banks that could not collect the money that was owed to them had to close their doors. Business failures became commonplace. Each new failure—each worker laid off—meant less spending, fewer jobs and more discouragement. Within two years there were 14 million workers unemployed.

Hoover Tried to Combat the Depression

President Hoover tried to restore confidence. He urged businessmen to keep wages as high as possible and to continue production. In order to put men to work, the President asked Congress to vote money for new roads and buildings. Congress set up a Reconstruction Finance Corporation to lend money to banks, railroads and factories. Congress also set up the Home Loan Bank to lend money at low interest to people who owed money on their homes. When the depression spread to Europe, President Hoover called off all war-debt payments for one year.

These measures show that President Hoover felt that the government is at least partially responsible for improving business conditions and saving people from disaster. Hoover was the first President to use this type of government action to fight a depression. Unfortunately these measures were not enough. Prices kept going down. More and more factories closed and unemployment increased.

FRANKLIN D. ROOSEVELT WON THE ELECTION OF 1932

The election of 1932 took place during the worst part of the depression. The Republican Party renominated Hoover, but they had little chance to win. The Democrats nominated Franklin D. Roosevelt, the Governor of New York. Roosevelt was a wealthy man who had been the Democratic candidate for Vice-President in 1920. Then he was stricken with polio and paralyzed. He fought back to health and was elected Governor of New York in 1928.

In their campaign the Democrats blamed the Republican Party for the depression. The Democrats also favored repeal of the Eighteenth Amendment. Roosevelt promised help for the farmers, new laws for railroads, new laws for banks, laws to control the stock market, and projects to give people jobs. He called his program a *New Deal*. He was elected.

Just before Roosevelt became President in March of 1933, the depression hit rock bottom. Nearly 15 million people were unemployed. All over the country, banks were closing. On his first day in office Roosevelt spoke over the radio. He said America had to face the facts but that "the only thing we have to fear is fear itself." The next day Roosevelt declared a "bank holiday" by ordering all banks in the nation to close their doors. Then he called Congress into a special session and proposed a new law to protect banks and to let sound banks open again. Roosevelt's bank bill had been prepared beforehand. It was passed by both houses of Congress and signed all in one day.

The Emergency Banking Relief Act gave the President power to regulate the value of money. It also provided for federal inspectors to go to each bank. If the bank was strong enough to resume business, it could reopen. Soon sound banks were operating. However, some banks could not be saved, and they remained closed. Depositors in these banks lost their savings. But the banking crisis was over.

THE NEW DEAL ENLARGED THE GOVERNMENT'S ROLE

The New Deal marked a turning point in American history. From 1933 on, the federal government did many things that had been left to the states. The problems raised by the depression were very complicated and they were nationwide. Thus separate states could not find solutions by acting alone.

The steps that made up the New Deal were of two kinds. First there were the laws that were passed to help end the depression. Many of these were temporary. Second, there were long-term reforms, many of which became permanent.

The Government Dealt with Business

Some of the new laws helped business, while others controlled it. Some laws put the government itself into business, and some provided direct help to individual citizens. Laws were passed so fast, and so many new government agencies were set up to enforce them, that it was hard to keep track of all of them.

After it helped the banks, the administration turned to the problems of business failures and unemployment. In June of 1933 Congress passed the National Industrial Recovery Act (NIRA). This Act allowed businessmen to get together and fix prices. However, the prices had to be approved by the government, and businessmen had to keep wages above a minimum level. The Act helped to raise prices, but it did not put many laborers back to work.

One way to help business is to put more money into circulation. This makes prices as well as wages go up, and it makes it easier for people to pay their debts. In order to do this, Congress passed the Gold Reserve Act that fixed the amount of gold in the dollar at about half of what it was before. Congress also gave the President power to buy American silver at a high price and pay for it by issuing new dollar bills. Both of these Acts put more money into circulation. Along with the Banking Act and the NIRA, these measures were intended to help business to recover from the depression.

Most New Deal laws aimed at controlling business and protecting the interests of the average man. Congress set up the Securities and Exchange Commission in 1934 in order to regulate the selling of stock. The purposes of the SEC were to protect people who bought stock and to prevent another stock market crash. The SEC also was given the power to regulate holding companies which had taken the place of trusts. Congress also set up the Federal Deposit Insurance Corporation. Through the FDIC the government insured all bank deposits up to the amount of $10,000. If banks failed, people would no longer lose all of their savings. Another act set up a Federal Communications Commission to regulate telephone, telegraph and broadcasting companies.

The New Deal also began to lower tariffs. In 1934 the Reciprocal Trade Agreements Act gave the President power to cut tariff rates in half for any country that would give the United States equal trade advantages. Since then tariff agreements have been made with most countries, and American tariffs have been getting lower.

Another long-range New Deal project was the Tennessee Valley Authority, or TVA. Congress set up the TVA to build dams, control floods and sell electricity in the Tennessee River valley. In effect this put the government into business and it drew much criticism. Some people thought that the government was going beyond its constitutional power. But the Supreme Court said that the TVA was constitutional. By supplying electricity and controlling floods in the Tennessee River valley, the TVA brought prosperity to the surrounding area. But the criticism continued.

The Government Helped the Unemployed

Meanwhile, something had to be done for people who were out of work and had no money. Congress set up a Federal Emergency Relief Administration. The FERA lent money to state and local governments to help pay for relief of the unemployed.

Congress also set up four agencies to create new jobs. The Public Works Administration enlarged the agency that President Hoover had started. The PWA built offices, court houses, dams and highways. It also lent money to local governments for public works. The Civilian Conservation Corps (CCC) gave jobs to young men. Men were employed by the government to plant trees, build roads and improve national parks. The National Youth Administration gave part-time work to students who were still in school. The Works Progress Administration furnished money for all kinds of projects. WPA artists painted murals in public buildings, WPA writers wrote guidebooks about national parks, WPA musicians gave concerts, and WPA actors put on plays. Critics claimed that much of this work was unnecessary and too expensive. They called it "boondoggling." But the projects did take many people off relief.

Congress also set up the Home Owners Loan Corporation. The HOLC lent money to home owners to help them pay off mortgages or pay for repairs to their houses.

The government agencies that gave aid directly to people in need were temporary. The HOLC ended in 1936, although the CCC lasted until 1942.

The Government Helped the Farmers

To help farmers, the New Deal began a program that became permanent. Even in the 1920's the farmers did not prosper because they raised more produce than they could sell. When the depression came, farmers were desperate. The New Deal set up a plan whereby the government would pay farmers to cut down their production. Congress passed the Agricultural Adjustment Act in 1933. Under this Act farmers could get money from the government for not raising crops. This Act was soon changed so that, in order to collect any payments, farmers had to plant crops that would save the soil. Later on the AAA was made permanent. Such a program is undoubtedly wasteful, but it has brought prosperity to the farmer. And, as yet, nobody has found a better way to do the same thing.

The Government Assisted Workers

The New Deal also passed laws that helped organized labor. Congress adopted the National Labor Relations Act in 1935. It is called the Wagner Act since Senator Robert Wagner of New York had proposed it. The Wagner Act forbade employers from punishing workers because they belonged to a union. All employers were required to deal with union leaders elected by the workers. A National Labor Relations Board was set up to enforce the Wagner Act. Another congressional law, the Fair Labor Standards Act, put a limit on the number of hours a laborer should work and fixed the minimum wage an employer could pay. Under these acts the labor movement grew to be large and powerful.

Perhaps the most important product of the New Deal was the Social Security Act. This Act set up a government-run insurance plan that is still in operation. Every worker covered by social security contributes a certain part of his pay to the Social Security Administration. Employers also contribute. From the money collected, retired men and women who have reached a certain age receive monthly payments until their death. Payments also are made to widows and children of workers who have died and to any disabled worker over fifty years of age. This part of the program is run directly by the federal government.

A second part of the social security program provides for payments to states. The states use this money to help run their own unemployment plans. Under a third part of the program, the federal government helps states to provide aid to disabled persons and needy children.

ROOSEVELT'S POLICIES PLEASED A MAJORITY OF THE VOTERS

The New Deal was unique in two ways. First of all, the federal government took bold action to combat the depression. It helped business on one hand, and controlled it on the other. Second, the federal government gave direct help to many people who had never been helped by the government before. New Deal laws gave help directly to farmers, to disabled people, to retired people, to unemployed people and to laborers in unions. The federal government had never done this before, except for veterans. The Constitution gave Congress the power to "provide for the general welfare." But formerly "the general welfare" had meant vaguely what was good for the country in general. The New Deal was based on the idea that the general welfare meant the welfare of the individual men and women who made up the nation. Critics of the New Deal thought this a mistake, and they objected to what they called "the welfare state."

Nearly all of the New Deal program was passed within a six-year period. To finance the New Deal, the government had to borrow money, thereby increasing the national debt. This meant that income taxes had to be raised. Yet, despite all of this spending, there were still more than 8 million people unemployed. Nevertheless, Roosevelt's program was popular with the voters. In 1936 Roosevelt was re-elected President by an overwhelming vote. He carried every state except two. The Republican candidate, Alfred M. Landon, carried only the states of Maine and Vermont.

Four years later, in 1940, Roosevelt ran for the presidency again. Previously, no American President had ever served more than two terms. To oppose the Democrats, the Republicans nominated their first "liberal" candidate since Theodore Roosevelt. His name was Wendell Willkie. Since many Republicans had accepted large parts of the New Deal by this time, there seemed little difference in the stands of the two parties. But the people broke tradition and elected Roosevelt to a third term.

Now the President had to face a new problem. The continent of Europe had already plunged into World War II.

REVIEW ACTIVITIES

1. Describe life in the United States during the 1920's. Why is this period known as the "mad decade?"
2. In what ways was the nation's economy unstable in the middle and late 1920's?
3. What measures did President Hoover take to end the depression? How successful were they?
4. How did Roosevelt's New Deal help the farmers? What

did the New Deal do for the workers and the unemployed?
5. What is Social Security? How does it help the unemployed and the needy?

Select the words that best complete the following sentences. (*Please do not write in this book.*)

1. The ———— Party came to power in 1921. It was in favor of ———— tariffs.
2. Hoover defeated ———— ———— for President in 1928, but because of the depression, the ———— Party won in 1932.
3. One day after he became President, Roosevelt declared a "———— ————." The ———— ———— ———— Act gave Roosevelt the power to regulate the value of money.
4. Two New Deal projects to help the country during the depression were the ———— ———— ———— Act, which allowed businessmen to fix prices at levels approved by the government, and the ———— ———— ———— ————, which lent money to state and local governments to help pay for the relief of the unemployed.
5. ———— ———— is the only President ever to be elected more than twice. In 1940, his opponent was ———— ————.

Who or what were the following:

1. Eighteenth Amendment
2. Calvin Coolidge
3. Reciprocal Trade Agreement
4. Tennessee Valley Authority
5. Agricultural Adjustment Act

CHAPTER 18

World War II

DICTATORS CHALLENGED THE DEMOCRACIES

World War II began in September of 1939. That is, the actual shooting began then. The stresses that led to war had been building up in Europe and Asia for some time.

In Europe the years following World War I were troubled ones. Economic problems gripped the continent, and they helped dictators to rise to power. The first such dictator to appear was Benito Mussolini of Italy.

Almost immediately after World War I, Italy was plunged into a severe depression. Strikes and violence swept the country. This situation gave Mussolini his chance. He and his Fascist Party gained control of the government in 1922.

Mussolini claimed that democracy could not solve Italy's problems. He said that the country needed strong leadership that could be provided only by one man with great power. He quickly set about getting that power for himself.

He outlawed all political parties that opposed him, forced the press to print what he told them to print and began to supervise nearly every type of economic activity. Then he started to build up the army and navy so that Italy could get colonies. In 1935 he attacked Ethiopia.

Hitler and the Nazis Controlled Germany

In Germany a similar situation developed. After losing the war, the Germans had set up a democratic government. But Germans were not used to democracy, and many of them lost faith in their government during the depression of the 1930's. They began to look for a strong leader.

Germany also had a Fascist party. Its members called themselves the National Socialists, or Nazis. They were led by Adolf Hitler, who had borrowed many of Mussolini's ideas. He told the German people that their leaders had betrayed them. He blamed all of Germany's problems on the Treaty of Versailles and the country's Jewish population. In 1933 Hitler became Chancellor of Germany.

Following Mussolini's example, Hitler quickly set up a dictatorship. He called himself the Fuehrer, or leader. His secret police, the Gestapo, arrested anyone who opposed him. The Jews were deprived of citizenship, beaten, imprisoned and even killed.

Then Hitler began to build up Germany's military might. He increased the size of the army and converted a large part of the country's industry to the production of war materials. In 1936 he sent troops into the Rhineland, a section of Germany next to France. All of these actions were forbidden by the Treaty of Versailles. Britain and France objected, but did not stop Hitler. They did not want war.

Civil war broke out in Spain in 1936. Germany and Italy helped the Spanish rebel leader, Francisco Franco. Franco defeated the democratic government of Spain and became a dictator like Mussolini and Hitler.

Meanwhile, in the Far Eastern country of Japan, another type of dictatorship was being set up. By 1931 military men had won control of the government. These men favored the expansion of Japanese influence by force. They felt that Japan should gain new markets and territories. They controlled the emperor and encouraged the people to worship him.

In 1931 Japan seized control of Manchuria, a province of China. The United States refused to recognize this illegal conquest but took no further action. Thus Japan was able to prepare for further aggression. In 1937 she launched an attack against the rest of China. Within two years Japanese armies occupied huge sections of Chinese territory.

While these events were taking place, most Americans were urging the United States to remain neutral. Public opinion in this country was strongly opposed to any action that could lead us into war. Between 1935 and 1937, Congress passed laws to keep America out of war. These laws said that Americans could not lend money or sell war materials to any country at war. American citizens could not travel on ships of any country that was at war. Finally, these laws said that Americans could not sell food or clothing or supplies to any country at war unless the deal was in cash. Such laws gave up the neutral rights that Americans had always stood for. But Americans were ready to go to great lengths to stay out of war. Meanwhile, the situation in Europe was becoming more and more dangerous.

WORLD WAR II BEGAN IN 1939

In 1938 Hitler sent his armies into Austria. The Austrians did not fight back, and their country was united with Germany. Then Germany took over a part of Czechoslovakia, also without a fight. Hitler's next goal was Poland. He signed a treaty with Stalin, the Russian dictator, to divide Poland. Stalin promised not to interfere if Hitler invaded that country. German armies attacked Poland on September 1, 1939. When this happened, Great Britain and France decided that they must act. Otherwise, Germany would take over all of Europe piece by piece. On September 3 England and France declared war on Germany, and World War II was underway.

Germany's army was large and well prepared. It conquered Poland within a few weeks. The English and French might have attacked Germany while Hitler's army was fighting the Poles, but they preferred not to. Instead, they waited all winter long behind fortifications on the French-German border. This gave Hitler a chance to strike in another direction. Moving swiftly, his troops occupied Denmark and fought their way well into Norway. Only then did the Germans attack France. They swept through the Netherlands and Belgium and crossed the Belgian border into France. The allied troops were defeated very quickly. The British retreated to Dunkirk, a port on the English Channel. From here a large part of their army was taken back to Britain by boat. In June of 1940, Italy entered the war on Germany's side. Mussolini's armies attacked France from the south. On June 22 the French surrendered.

Hitler's armies now occupied Poland, Denmark, Norway, the Netherlands, Belgium and France. Factories in these countries were forced to help the German war effort. People were denied their freedom. Jews were hunted down and sent to concentration camps. Millions of them were killed. Only England remained to fight the Nazi armies.

The United States Helped England and Russia

When Americans saw that Germany might conquer England, they knew that democracy in America was in danger. Congress voted money to build up our military strength and passed another Selective Service Act. This law said that young men could be drafted into the armed forces. It was America's first peacetime draft. Early in the war, Roosevelt had urged Congress to let the democratic countries buy arms in the United States. At the time, many people objected. As German victories increased, however, most Americans began to agree with Roosevelt. Americans started selling arms to England and France. Finally, when Britain stood alone against Hitler, Roosevelt took further action. He transferred military equipment to private companies who then sold it to the British. He also agreed to exchange fifty American destroyers for a lease on eight naval and air bases in the Atlantic Ocean. The British were still holding out in 1941, but they were running short of money. President Roosevelt proposed that America lend the British whatever supplies they needed to carry on the war. America agreed to sell on credit all the materials Great Britain needed. Payment would be made after the war was over. In addition, the American navy spread out in the North Atlantic Ocean in order to protect ships that carried goods to England.

The German leaders knew that only American goods made it possible for England to hold out. They said they would attack American ships. In May of 1941 German submarines began to sink American merchant vessels. In October, 1941, they even attacked our warships. The danger of war became greater.

Most Americans saw the danger and supported President Roosevelt, but there were others who opposed him. Some of these people were *pacifists*. They believed that all wars were wrong. A few Americans even thought that Germany and Hitler were right. Other Americans were *isolationists*. They said that Hitler would not attack America and that the war in Europe was not a threat to our security. They believed that the United States could get along without the rest of the world. There was enough isolationist feeling in the country to prevent the United States from declaring war.

Meanwhile, in June, 1941, German armies suddenly attacked Russia. They soon occupied a large part of Russian territory. Americans did not like the Communist dictatorship in Russia any more than they liked Hitler's dictatorship in Germany. But the United States decided that the first thing to do was to defeat Germany. Since Russia was also fighting Germany, we sent aid to Russia.

In August of 1941 President Roosevelt and Prime Minister Churchill of Great Britain met on a naval ship in the North Atlantic. They drew up an agreement known as the Atlantic Charter. They agreed that no country should gain any territory from the war. They also agreed that the Nazis must be destroyed, and that people everywhere should have the right to choose their own government.

The Attack on Pearl Harbor Ended American Neutrality

In the Far East, Japanese armies were still fighting in China. In September, 1940, Japan had signed a pact with Germany and Italy. The three countries agreed to come to one another's aid if any one of them was attacked by a country not already in the war. This meant that Japan could expect help from Germany and Italy if her policies brought her into a war with the United States. With this assurance, the Japanese continued their aggression. In 1940 they took over Indochina and threatened to take over Thailand.

President Roosevelt tried economic pressure to halt the Japanese advances. He made it practically impossible for Japan to trade with the United States. Japanese-American relations became very strained. A series of negotiations was held, but no agreement was reached. The United States insisted that Japan get out of China, but the Japanese refused. On Sunday morning, December 7, 1941, the Japanese struck without warning. Japanese planes bombed the

American naval base at Pearl Harbor in the Hawaiian Islands. This raid destroyed a large part of our Pacific fleet. Congress immediately declared war on Japan. A few days later Germany and Italy declared war on us.

THE UNITED STATES AND HER ALLIES WON THE WAR

For several months the Japanese advance in the Pacific went practically unchecked. The American navy had been greatly weakened at Pearl Harbor, and it could do little to stop the enemy. Guam and Wake Island fell despite heroic resistance by American troops. The Japanese invaded the Philippines, and the Americans were forced to surrender after months of bitter fighting. Before the surrender, President Roosevelt ordered General Douglas MacArthur, our commander in the Philippine Islands, to go to Australia. There MacArthur took command of American, Australian and New Zealand troops. It was his job to organize the fight to drive the Japanese back. But it was a long time before the allied forces were able to take the offensive in the Pacific.

On the other side of the world, Hitler had extended his control into North Africa. German and Italian troops were pushing across the desert into Egypt. Should they conquer Egypt, they would control the Suez Canal. This canal forms a vital link in the transportation route between Britain and the rich oil fields on the Persian Gulf. Its loss would have cut off a large part of Britain's oil supply. Moreover, it would have given the Germans nearly complete control of North Africa and the Mediterannean Sea. The British were fighting desperately for survival.

At the same time, other German armies were pushing deeper into Russia. Hitler's troops were at the gates of Moscow. Farther south they threatened Stalingrad and southern Russia. During 1942 it seemed that the Axis powers of Germany, Italy and Japan could not be stopped. But the tide of their victories was soon held back by superior forces.

America Prepared for a Long Struggle

The attack on Pearl Harbor ended isolationist feelings in the United States. The country quickly prepared for war. Men were taken into the armed forces as fast as they could be trained. Before the war was over, 10 million men were in the army and 4 million were in the navy. Women joined the armed forces to help with jobs that did not involve actual fighting.

The war cost enormous amounts of money. Income taxes were increased. To make sure that these taxes were paid, Congress required employers to deduct them from pay checks. However, more than half of the cost of war was met by borrowing money. When the war began, the United States government was 43 billion dollars in debt. When the war ended, the national debt was 259 billion dollars.

During the war all of the government's efforts were directed toward winning the struggle. The New Deal was forgotten. Big business, labor and government all co-operated. Industry had to produce war materials. Farms had to produce as much grain as possible. Goods and men had to be transported to market or to the armed forces overseas. To organize all of this activity, many new government agencies were set up. The War Production Board helped factories to get raw materials. The Office of Defense Transportation kept the railroads running efficiently and saw to it that goods were moved as fast as possible. The War Manpower Commission helped factories and war industries to get the workmen they needed. The National War Labor Board worked with unions and factory owners to keep the country free from strikes. Congress even gave the government power to operate factories in the event of a strike. An Office of Price Administration kept prices from going too high. An Office of Food Administration made certain that people did not buy food that was needed abroad or in the armed forces. Food, fuel oil and gasoline were rationed.

As a result of these measures, the United States was able to send vast quantities of goods to England and Russia. We were also able to send a powerful army into the field.

The Allies Won in Africa and Invaded Italy

President Roosevelt and Prime Minister Churchill had agreed that it was most important to defeat Germany first. They set up a military staff to plan for the armies of both nations. It was agreed first to get the Germans out of North Africa. In July of 1942 the British army in Egypt, commanded by General George Montgomery, attacked the German armies under General Rommel. Then in November the allied forces, under General Dwight D. Eisenhower, landed in Morocco at the opposite end of North Africa. In May, 1943, after a winter of bitter fighting, the Germans were forced to surrender.

Two months later allied armies launched an attack against Italy and captured Sicily. With their homeland invaded, the Italians turned on Mussolini and forced him to flee. The Italian government wanted to make peace, but German armies would not allow this. They remained in Italy and kept on fighting. In September, 1943, American soldiers under General Mark Clark landed at Salerno and Anzio near Naples. They faced strong German resistance and fought a bloody battle. It was almost a year before they could get as far as Rome.

The Allied Leaders Met to Plan the War

While the fighting in Italy was going on, allied leaders met to plan the war. In January, 1943, soon after American troops had landed in North Africa, Roosevelt and Churchill met at Casablanca. Here they agreed on the terms for Germany—unconditional surrender!

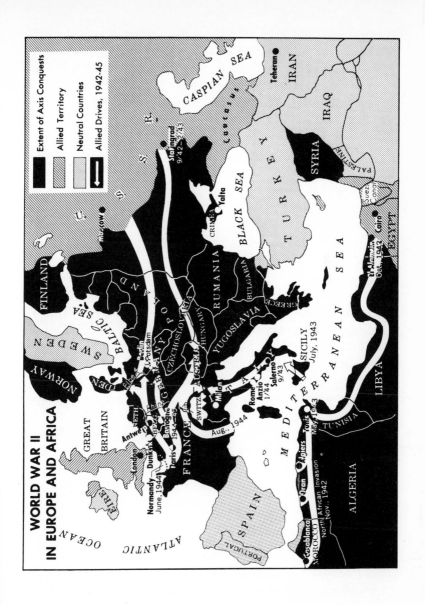

WORLD WAR II
IN EUROPE AND AFRICA

Extent of Axis Conquests
Allied Territory
Neutral Countries
Allied Drives, 1942-45

In the fall of 1943, Roosevelt and Churchill met with Chiang Kai-shek, the leader of China. They promised China that when Japan surrendered, all the territory taken from China would be returned. Then Roosevelt and Churchill went to Teheran, the capital of Iran, to meet with Joseph Stalin of Russia. Here the three leaders laid plans to invade France.

Allied Forces Closed in on Germany

During 1943 American and British airplanes began to bomb German industrial cities. An enormous army was built up in the British Isles. Finally, on June 6, 1944, D-Day, the allied forces commanded by General Eisenhower, invaded France on the beaches of Normandy. The Germans had been weakened further by the war in Russia, and they were caught by surprise. Within a few weeks the allied beachhead in France was secure. American and British soldiers broke through the German lines. With the help of loyal Frenchmen, they spread out all over northern France.

In eastern Europe, German armies were losing. Russian forces stopped them at Stalingrad and slowly drove them back into Poland. By the end of 1944, the Germans had been driven back almost to the borders of Germany itself. In December the Germans tried to break through the American line in northern France, but they failed. German fighting power seemed almost gone. Her cities and industries were destroyed by allied bombers. Her oil supplies were used up. But Hitler would not surrender.

Roosevelt, Stalin and Churchill Met at Yalta

When election time came in 1944, the Democrats nominated Roosevelt once again. Roosevelt defeated the Republican candidate, Thomas Dewey, and became President for a fourth term.

In February, 1945, President Roosevelt attended his final

meeting with Churchill and Stalin. He met them at Yalta in southern Russia. By this time the Russian armies had driven the Germans back. Russian armies were in Poland, Hungary and Romania. They set up Communist governments. Roosevelt and Churchill wanted Russia to hold democratic elections. Russia promised. They wanted Russia to join the war against Japan. Russia promised. In return, Roosevelt and Churchill agreed that Russia should get part of Poland. Many people thought the Russians were given too much at Yalta. Actually, the Russians were already in eastern Europe. There was little else that Roosevelt and Churchill could do.

Soon after Roosevelt returned from Yalta, he died while resting at Warm Springs, Georgia. On April 12, 1945, Vice-President Harry S. Truman became President.

Germany Surrendered

In the spring of 1945, American and British armies crossed the Rhine, and Russian armies entered eastern Germany. The Germans fought desperately, but their defense collapsed. In May American and Russian forces met in central Germany. Hitler committed suicide. The German armies surrendered. War in Europe was over. The allies were free to throw all of their strength against Japan.

American Forces Pushed Across the Pacific

The Japanese advance in the Pacific had already been stopped. During 1942 and 1943 the United States Navy had won important victories in the Coral Sea, Midway Island, Guadalcanal and the Bismarck Sea. These victories enabled American forces to start an "island hopping" drive toward Japan itself. One by one, islands in the Pacific were invaded and taken. Each island provided a base of operations for the next attack.

By October, 1944, the troops under General MacArthur

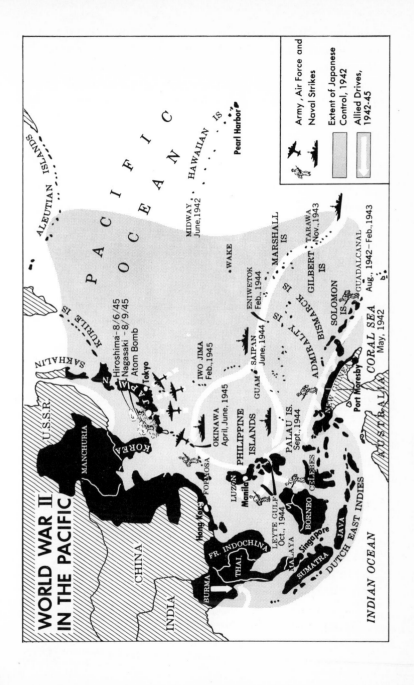

WORLD WAR II
IN THE PACIFIC

Army, Air Force and Naval Strikes

Extent of Japanese Control, 1942

Allied Drives, 1942-45

INDIAN OCEAN

INDIA

CHINA

U.S.S.R.

MANCHURIA

KOREA

JAPAN

Tokyo

Hiroshima - 8/6/45
Nagasaki - 8/9/45
Atom Bomb

SAKHALIN

KURILE IS.

ALEUTIAN ISLANDS

PACIFIC OCEAN

HAWAIIAN IS.

Pearl Harbor

MIDWAY, June, 1942

WAKE

IWO JIMA
Feb.,1945

OKINAWA
April, June, 1945

FORMOSA

Hong Kong

BURMA

THAI.

FR. INDOCHINA

MALAYA

Singapore

SUMATRA

BORNEO

CELEBES

JAVA

DUTCH EAST INDIES

PHILIPPINE
ISLANDS

LUZON

Manila

LEYTE GULF
Oct., 1944

PALAU IS.
Sept., 1944

GUAM

SAIPAN
June, 1944

ENIWETOK
Feb., 1944

MARSHALL
IS

GILBERT
IS

TARAWA
Nov.,1943

ADMIRALTY
IS

BISMARCK
IS

SOLOMON
IS.

GUADALCANAL
Aug., 1942 – Feb., 1943

Port Moresby

CORAL SEA
May, 1942

AUSTRALIA

were ready to invade the Philippines. The Japanese navy was driven off, and American troops landed on Leyte and Samar. By February, 1945, Manila was recaptured. In that same month, American Marines captured the tiny island of Iwo Jima. From Iwo Jima American airplanes could bomb Japanese industries. The next island was Okinawa, close to the Japanese mainland. During the fighting for Okinawa, Japanese suicide pilots destroyed many American ships.

The Atomic Bomb Helped End the War

Meanwhile, American scientists had invented the atomic bomb. Early in the war, President Roosevelt had set teams of American and British scientists to work on atomic warfare. In July of 1945, they had the first bomb ready. By that time the war in Europe was over. The Japanese had been driven back almost to their home islands. Japan's cities were being bombed, and she was cut off from her supplies of food and raw materials. But the Japanese army refused to give up.

An invasion of Japan itself would have cost many American lives. President Truman decided to use the atomic bomb to bring the war to a quick end. So, on August 6, 1945, an American airplane dropped an atomic bomb on the Japanese city of Hiroshima. In a moment, the bomb wiped out the entire city and killed or injured 160,000 human beings. Two days later, Russian armies invaded Manchuria, the Japanese province in northern China. On August 9 another atomic bomb was exploded over the port of Nagasaki. The Japanese asked for peace. On September 2, 1945, Japan surrendered and World War II was over.

REVIEW ACTIVITIES

1. What aid did the United States give to Russia, France and England before we entered World War II? Why did the

United States think it important to help these countries?

2. What were the arguments against the United States giving aid to the above-mentioned countries?
3. Who attended the Yalta Conference? What decisions were reached at that meeting?
4. Why did Japan attack the United States?
5. Why did the United States use the atomic bomb? Where was it used?

Select the words that best complete the following sentences. (*Please do not write in this book.*)

1. Nazi Germany's ally in Europe was ——————. These countries were not democracies; they were ————.
2. When German armies invaded ———— in 1939, England and ———— declared war on Germany.
3. On December 7, 1941, the attack on ———— ———— ended American neutrality. Congress immediately declared war on ————.
4. Early in 1943 Roosevelt and ———— met at Casablanca. They agreed to demand an ———— surrender from Germany.
5. On June 6, 1944, which is known as ————, allied forces invaded the coast of ————.

Who or what were the following:

1. Benito Mussolini
2. Adolf Hitler
3. Atlantic Charter
4. Douglas MacArthur
5. Dwight D. Eisenhower

CHAPTER **19**

America and the World Today

COMMUNISM THREATENED THE FREE WORLD

After World War II there was no danger to America and her allies from Germany or Japan. The Nazis and the Japanese warlords were gone. But a new concern arose. Communism threatened the entire free world.

During the war Communist Russia and the democratic countries had fought side by side. They did not believe in the same things, but they worked together because they all opposed Hitler.

Communists do not believe in democratic government. They do not believe in freedom of the individual as we do. Where they are in control, they permit neither free speech, a free press nor the right to a speedy trial by jury. And they do not believe in capitalism, or free enterprise. They do not allow any private person to own a business and make a profit. They believe that all factories—that is, all "means of production"—should be owned by everybody together. Ownership and profits, they say, belong to society. Under communism, factories are owned and run by the state.

In America we believe that only a few things should be run this way—the post office system, which is run by the federal government; the public schools, which are run locally; and sometimes a bus line or subway system, which are run locally. A few city governments in the United States also own power plants to produce and sell electricity, and the federal government runs the TVA. But that is about all.

This difference of opinion as to who should own property and who should get profits is only half of the picture. Communists, especially those in Russia, are sure that anybody who believes in democracy and private profits will not accept the ideas of communism. So the Communists use force to make people believe in their system. They even deny freedom of speech and thought to their own people.

During the war the differences between communism and democracy did not seem as important as they did later. As long as the war continued, Russia and the democratic western countries worked together. And they planned ways for all nations to co-operate when the war was over.

The United States Helped to Found the United Nations

In April, 1945, men from fifty nations met at San Francisco and drew up the plan for the United Nations. The United Nations has six parts. There is the General Assembly where every nation is represented. At this Assembly, any question concerning world peace may be discussed. The Assembly brings problems into the open and makes recommendations. There is a Security Council that has only eleven members. In this Council, Russia, the United States, Great Britain, France and Nationalist China are always members. Six other nations are elected to the Council for terms of two years each. The Council appears to have strong powers, but it can act only if all five of the permanent members agree. One permanent member can stop any action by voting "no." This is known as the veto power.

The United Nations also includes an Economic and Social Council that studies living conditions all over the world. It recommends methods for raising the standard of living. The Trusteeship Council checks on the governments of territories that are run by larger nations. An International Court of Justice decides legal disputes between nations that agree to submit their disputes to the Court. Finally, there is an office force. This is the Secretariat which keeps the machinery moving. It is headed by the Secretary General. The headquarters of the United Nations are in New York City.

The Senate of the United States voted to accept this plan and become a member of the United Nations. You will remember that after World War I, the Senate turned down the League of Nations. This time it was different. Most Americans now realized that our country was tied up with world affairs. The vote in the Senate was 89 to 2 in favor of the United Nations.

It was not the United Nations, however, but the allied nations that had to decide on peace terms for Germany and Japan. Here the differences between Communist Russia and the democratic allies made things difficult. At the end of the war Germany was divided into four sections which were occupied by troops from Russia, Great Britain, the United States and France. Also, the former capital of Germany, Berlin, was divided into four parts. Allied soldiers were to stay in Germany until a peace treaty was worked out. But Russia and the other allied powers were never able to agree on a peace treaty.

Russia Set Up Communist Governments in Eastern Europe

Russia wanted Germany to pay huge sums in coal, food and machinery. Russia also wanted Germany to remain a divided country. Russian troops and Communist officials made the Russian section of East Germany into a Communist zone. They would not let Germany become one country unless it was all Communist. The other powers in Germany let their three sections join together into one democratic state. This is the Federal Republic of Germany that we call West Germany.

Elsewhere in Europe, Russia set up other Communist governments. She did this in Romania, Bulgaria, Yugoslavia, Hungary and Poland. The free elections that Stalin had promised were never held. Then Communist workers and soldiers began to move into Greece and Turkey. Greece asked the United Nations for help. However, Russia used her veto in the Security Council and the United Nations could not act.

The Truman Doctrine and the Marshall Plan Helped Western Europe

At this point President Truman decided that the United States should help Greece. He said that the United States would support free people everywhere who resisted communism. This policy became known as the Truman Doctrine. In 1947 Congress voted 400 million dollars to give military aid to Greece and Turkey. This helped these countries to resist the Communist attacks and to remain free.

The United States took other steps to oppose communism in Western Europe. Many West European countries had been weakened by the war and were suffering from poverty and unemployment. Communist supporters urged the poor people and the unemployed to vote for communism.

The United States worked out a plan to help restore trade, build up farms and factories and reduce unemployment in these countries. This was the European Recovery Program, sometimes called the Marshall Plan because it was first proposed by the American Secretary of State, George Marshall.

Congress voted millions of dollars to put the Marshall Plan into operation. As a result, business conditions in Western Europe improved. The people kept their political freedom and did not turn to communism.

America and Her Allies Created NATO

While the spread of communism however, was checked for the moment, the threat of Russian military expansion still remained. Consequently, the United States agreed to enter into an alliance for Western Europe's defense. Never before in peacetime had we signed a military treaty with European countries. Until World War II America believed in "no entangling alliances." But America could no longer defend democracy alone. So in 1946 the United States helped to form the North Atlantic Treaty Organization, or NATO. Actually, NATO is more than a treaty. It is an organization that has an army of its own. At the present time fifteen nations are NATO members. The United States, Great Britain, Canada, France, Belgium, Holland, Luxembourg, Italy, Denmark, Norway, Iceland and Portugal all signed the agreement in 1949. In 1952 Greece and Turkey joined NATO. West Germany became a member in 1955.

Communism Expanded in Asia

In Asia the same struggle between democracy and communism took place, and the United States became involved. First, there was the problem of Japan. The Japanese had to set up a new government. We urged them to choose democracy rather than communism, and we were successful. By the time General MacArthur's occupation forces were ready to leave Japan, the Japanese were well on the road to democratic self-government. Japan and the United States signed a peace treaty in September, 1951.

But China fell to the Communists. The Nationalist Government of Chiang Kai-shek was not able to bring order and prosperity to China. Many Chinese people turned against Chiang. Chinese Communists began a war against Chiang's government. By 1949 the Communists had won, and all that remained of free China was the Island of Formosa. China became a Communist country.

Korea became half Communist and half democratic. At the end of the war, allied soldiers from the democratic countries occupied the southern half of Korea; Communist troops from Russia occupied the northern half. In 1950 the Communists tried to take over the entire country by force. The case came before the United Nations, and the General Assembly voted to oppose the Communists by force. America sent soldiers, planes and guns to Korea. The United Nations troops were commanded by General MacArthur. After more than two years of bitter fighting, the war came to an end. The Communists retained control of North Korea, but the Republic of South Korea remained free.

SEATO Was Formed to Stop Communist Expansion in the Far East

Almost immediately the Chinese Communists began to spread out into Southeast Asia. They took over the northern part of Indochina. To stop them from expanding further, the United States joined the Southeast Asian Treaty Organization. SEATO is a defense pact for Asia that operates in much the same way as NATO. Its members include Britain, France, Australia, Pakistan, Thailand and the Philippines. Through SEATO the United States can give military aid to countries like Vietnam in their struggle against communism. The United States also has taken non-military steps to help fight communism in Asia. American experts have been sent to help Asian countries improve their farming, manufacturing and schooling. In addition, the United States had helped to keep Communist China from becoming a member of the United Nations.

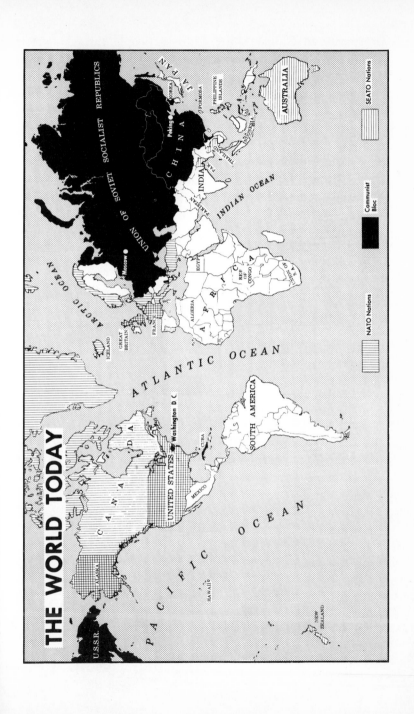

THE WORLD TODAY

U.S.S.R.

ARCTIC OCEAN

UNION OF SOVIET SOCIALIST REPUBLICS

Moscow

JAPAN

KOREA

FORMOSA

CHINA

Peking

INDIA

PAKISTAN

THAILAND

PHILIPPINE ISLANDS

INDONESIA

INDIAN OCEAN

AUSTRALIA

ICELAND

GREAT BRITAIN

FRANCE

ALGERIA

EGYPT

AFRICA

REP. OF CONGO

KENYA

ATLANTIC OCEAN

CANADA

ALASKA

UNITED STATES

Washington D C

MEXICO

CUBA

SOUTH AMERICA

PACIFIC OCEAN

HAWAII

NEW ZEALAND

NATO Nations

Communist Bloc

SEATO Nations

**Fear of Communism Led to Loyalty Investigations
in the United States**

The United States opposed the spread of communism everywhere, but it was not successful in Mainland China, North Korea or Eastern Europe. This failure disturbed many Americans. They began to think that America was being betrayed to the Communists. Their fears were supported when a few Russian spies were discovered and convicted. The government then began to test the loyalty of all important government workers. Communist Party leaders were tried and put in jail for wanting to overthrow the government. But the hunt for Communists went much further. Private companies looked for Communists among their employees. In the Senate, the Committee on Government Operations looked for Communists in all government departments. The chairman of this committee was Senator Joseph McCarthy of Wisconsin. McCarthy accused many people of Communist beliefs, but his committee uncovered little evidence. In time many Americans resented his irresponsible tactics. Eventually even his fellow senators condemned his unbecoming conduct. After this, McCarthy's influence declined and the hunt for Communists died down. It was clear that the vast majority of Americans were loyal citizens. Meanwhile, the United States was enjoying greater prosperity than it had ever known before.

AMERICANS FACED NEW CHALLENGES AFTER WORLD WAR II

America had recovered quickly from World War II. The change from producing war materials to producing consumer goods did not cause unemployment. The government ended price controls in 1946 and prices went up by about 25 per cent, but inflation did not get out of hand. Returning soldiers found jobs. Others were trained for new jobs at government expense. In 1944 Congress had passed the G.I. Bill of Rights that gave money to veterans who wanted to attend school or train for a new job. Congress also passed laws that made it possible for veterans to borrow money at a low interest rate to buy a house or start a business. The army was cut from 14 million men to 2 million, but the government continued to spend a lot of money on defense. The atom bomb program was costly. Jet planes, rockets and atomic submarines were added to our forces. With all this spending, business continued to grow. The country did not have a depression like the one that followed World War I.

Truman's Program Met with Opposition in Congress

When the first post-war election came in 1948, the Democratic Party nominated President Truman for a second term. But the Democrats were divided. Northern Democrats wanted the party to take a firm stand in favor of civil rights. They wished to support laws that would make sure all Negroes would have the right to vote, the right to fair trials and to a good education. Many southern Democrats objected to this stand. Some of them formed a Dixiecrat Party with a separate candidate. Still other Democrats thought Truman was too conservative, and they organized the Progressive Party. With the Democrats divided, the Republicans were sure of victory. They nominated Thomas E. Dewey, the Governor of New York, who had been their candidate in 1944. However, President Truman was re-elected.

Truman wanted Congress to pass several laws similar to those of the New Deal. He wanted compulsory health insurance, and he wanted to include more people under social security. He wanted the government to build dams to produce electricity on the Missouri and Columbia Rivers. He wanted federal aid to education, a higher minimum wage and laws that were more favorable to labor unions. But little of Truman's program was passed. Conservative southern

Democrats joined with Republicans in voting against it. The war in Korea was the main event of Truman's second term.

Eisenhower Served As President for Eight Years

By 1952 the country was ready for a change. The Republicans nominated a popular war hero, General Dwight D. Eisenhower. General Eisenhower had commanded the allied forces in Europe. After the war he had become President of Columbia University. He was popular and he had no political enemies. In the election he defeated the Democratic candidate, Adlai Stevenson. President Eisenhower proved to be in favor of social security, public housing, aid to education and federal aid to states for roads, hospitals and other public works. Four years later, he was re-elected.

After the war the two major American political parties did not seem to differ very much. Both parties agreed that the United States should take a firm stand against Russia. Both parties accepted the idea of social security and the reforms of the New Deal. Both accepted the idea of tariffs based on reciprocal trade agreements. Both agreed that the federal government had a responsibility for the welfare of the people. And both parties agreed that civil rights should be extended to every American citizen, regardless of his religion or the color of his skin. Still, the two parties differed somewhat in their approach. In general it may be said that the Democrats wanted the federal government to do more than the Republicans wanted it to do. The Democrats were less eager than Republicans to control powerful labor unions. In addition, the Democrats favored liberal federal spending, while the Republicans wanted to hold spending down.

Kennedy Was Elected in 1960

At the end of Eisenhower's second term, the Republican Party named Vice-President Richard Nixon as its candidate for President. The Democrats chose Senator John F.

Kennedy of Massachusetts. During the campaign the two candidates debated the issues in a series of television programs. For the first time in history nearly every voter had a chance to hear and see the candidates speak for themselves. In a very close election Kennedy won. Thus he became the first Roman Catholic to be President of the United States.

Congress Sought to Regulate Labor Unions

Although labor and management had co-operated for the national good during the war, the return of peace brought new problems in the area of labor relations. Organized labor had become powerful. Labor leaders could plan a nationwide strike that would affect all of the American people. In 1946 a coal strike lasted so long that the nation faced a winter without power or heat. The federal government seized control of the mines until an agreement could be reached. When the miners walked out on a new strike, President Truman used wartime powers and brought the union leaders into court. A federal court fined the union 3½ million dollars. In order to combat a railroad strike, Truman even asked Congress for power to draft workers into the army. Labor unions became so powerful that many people thought they should be controlled in the same way that the government controlled big business.

After the Republicans won control of Congress in 1946, they passed the Taft-Hartley Act. The purpose of this Act was to keep unions from growing too powerful. It provided that the unions could not force an employer to hire only union members. However, they could insist that a worker join the union within a short time after he started to work. Thus the *closed shop* became illegal, but the *union shop* was allowed. The Taft-Hartley Act also said that unions could not charge extremely high dues or compel an employer to hire more workers than he needed. Finally, the law provided that the President and the courts could halt a strike for eighty days, if it threatened an essential industry.

Although unions still had the power to conduct nation-wide strikes, labor leaders said that the Taft-Hartley Act was unfair. Most employers believed that the new law would set up a good balance between labor and management. Unions could not get Congress to repeal the Taft-Hartley Act.

Within the next years, unions faced even more restrictions. During the 1950's several states passed "right to work" laws that made even the union shop illegal. Then the courts learned that several union leaders were corrupt, and a congressional committee found out that many unions were undemocratic. Because of this, Congress passed the Landrum-Griffith Act to protect union members from dishonest leaders. The law required unions to make their account books public, and to hold their elections by secret ballot.

As yet, no one has found a way to create a perfect balance between labor and management. But the laws passed by Congress indicate that the public believes that it is just as important to control unions as it is to control big business.

The public responsibility of both unions and business ownership became an issue in 1962. When steel companies sought to raise their prices, President Kennedy brought pressure to stop them. He also warned labor leaders that they should not make wage demands that would increase prices.

Measures Were Taken to Guarantee Civil Rights

Another national problem that reappeared soon after World War II was that of civil rights. The United States is a democracy, and its Constitution entitles every citizen to certain rights. These are the right to vote, to speak freely, to hold meetings, to have a fair and speedy trial, and the right to equal treatment under the law. All citizens have these rights, but in practice not everyone has the same chance to use them. This is especially true of many Negroes in the

United States, particularly those who live in the Deep South.

Before and after the Civil War, the Republican Party was the champion of the Negroes. After the reconstruction period, however, southern states were left to do much as they pleased. Negroes often were discouraged from voting. In most southern states Negroes were sent to separate schools, made to use separate public rooms and forced to take separate seats on buses. This practice is known as *segregation*.

The issue of segregation became acute in 1954. In that year the Supreme Court decided that separate schools for Negro children and white children did not give Negroes equal rights. The Court ordered city and county governments all over the country to end segregation in the schools. To many white people in the South, this seemed revolutionary and dangerous. But gradually the changes were begun. Sometimes, as in Little Rock, Arkansas, there was resistance. Army troops were used to force the high school in Little Rock to accept Negro students. In time, segregation was ended in Louisville, Kentucky; Baltimore, Maryland; Nashville, Tennessee; Atlanta, Georgia, and Washington, D.C. Several southern colleges also began to admit Negroes. But when Negro student James Meredith enrolled at the University of Mississippi in 1962, the Governor of Mississippi tried to stop him. Riots broke out on the University's campus. Army troops and federal marshals had to protect Meredith's life.

Meanwhile, Negroes in the South demanded other rights. Negroes refused to ride in buses and streetcars until they were allowed to take any seat they pleased. Students sat down in restaurants and remained there until they were waited on or arrested.

In 1957 Congress set up a Civil Rights Commission to look into places where Negroes had been denied the right to vote because of their color. In 1960 Congress gave the federal government the right to use the courts to help these Negroes. Many sections in the South continued to resist the idea of equality in voting. But there was at least one sign of progress for the Negro. In the election of 1962, a Negro was elected to the state legislature of Georgia.

The Government Took Steps to Help Farmers and Increase Our Foreign Trade

Two other areas of national concern during the post-war years were the farm problem and foreign trade. The federal government had continued the New Deal plan for dealing with over-production on the farms. Both the Democratic and Republican administrations continued to make payments to farmers in return for their cutting down on production. Both parties also supported the idea of reciprocal trade agreements to lower tariffs. Then in 1962 Congress gave the President power by which he could practically eliminate protective tariffs altogether. This was the most important piece of tariff legislation since the New Deal.

The Conquest of Space Began During the Late 1950's

Perhaps the most sensational happening of the 1950's was the conquest of space. The space age began in October of 1957 when Russian scientists launched a rocket that put a small capsule, or satellite, into orbit, whirling around the earth. A few months later the United States did the same thing.

In 1961 the Russians sent a satellite with a man in it into orbit around the earth. The first American satellite to orbit the earth with a man aboard was launched early in 1962. Preparations began for a manned-flight to the moon.

A Communist Dictatorship Was Set Up in Cuba

Meanwhile the rivalry between Russian communism and western democracy came to within ninety miles of the United States. In 1959 Fidel Castro and his followers overthrew the dictatorial government of Cuba. Americans hoped that Castro would bring true democracy to Cuba, but Castro chose communism instead. He took over American sugar mills and other property in Cuba without paying for them. He brought Communist experts into Cuba and signed trade agreements with Russia.

Americans knew that a Communist foothold in Cuba was a danger to the United States. Americans stopped buying sugar from Cuba, and Congress passed a law making it illegal for Americans to trade with Cuba. This policy hurt Cuba's economy, but Castro remained in power.

In March of 1961, soon after Kennedy became President, a military expedition against Castro was organized by Cubans in the United States. The American government let the expedition sail but did not give it military support. The invasion failed.

President Kennedy Ordered a Blockade of the Cuban Coast

Then late in 1962, just before election time, the situation in Cuba became critical. Russian experts were setting up rocket bases in Cuba. These rockets could carry atomic bombs into the United States.

President Kennedy announced that the United States Navy would stop all ships from going to Cuba and prevent the landing of any more Russian rockets. He also warned Russia that if any missiles were fired from Cuba, America would consider this an attack by Russia. The missile bases, said President Kennedy, must be abolished.

The United Nations endeavored to bring about a peaceful end to the dispute. In the face of the strong action taken by President Kennedy, the Russian missile bases were torn down and the weapons were returned to Russia.

For the time being the Communists were unable to use Cuba as a military base. But the presence of the Castro government in Cuba remains an important factor in the continuing world struggle against communism.

REVIEW ACTIVITIES

1. What are the main differences between democracy and communism?
2. What are the three main parts of the United Nations?
3. What problems have labor unions created for the nation? How were union powers limited after 1946?
4. What are civil rights? How are they connected with segregation?
5. What major steps has the United States taken to check the spread of communism?

Select the words that best complete the following sentences. (*Please do not write in this book.*)

1. The Russians made East Germany into a _____ zone. England, the United States and France let their three sections of Western Germany combine into one _____ state.
2. The _____ Doctrine and the _____ Plan provided for United States military and economic aid to Western Europe.
3. The _____ _____ _____ Organization is a military alliance for Western Europe's defense. It has an _____ of its own.
4. At the end of the Korean conflict, the _____ retained control of North Korea, but the _____ of _____ _____ remained free.
5. A defense pact was set up for _____ that operates in much the same way as NATO. It is known as the _____ _____ _____ Organization.

Who were the following:

1. Harry Truman
2. Chiang Kai-shek
3. Joseph McCarthy
4. James Meredith
5. Fidel Castro